THE FUTURE OF THE
SACRAMENT OF PENANCE

THE FUTURE OF THE SACRAMENT OF PENANCE

Frank O'Loughlin

Paulist Press
New York/Mahwah, NJ

First published in 2007 by St Pauls Publications
Strathfield, Australia.

Cover design by Max Berry

Cover Image from www.dreamstime.com

Library of Congress Cataloging-in-Publication Data:

O'Loughlin, Frank.
    The future of the sacrament of penance / Frank O'Loughlin.
      p. cm.
    ISBN 978-0-8091-4556-0   (alk. paper)
    1. Penance — History. 2. Confession — Catholic Church. 3.
Reconciliation — Religious aspects — Catholic Church. I. Title.
    BX2260.O56 2009
    264´.02086 — dc22

                                                    2008024953

Published in 2009 by
Paulist Press
997 Macarthur Boulevard
Mahwah, New Jersey, 07430

www.paulistpress.com

Printed and bound in the
United States of America

Contents

Introduction

There is no doubt that Jesus called his first disciples, and calls us, to conversion. This is a core thread of the gospel, the Good News, that he proclaimed and lived.

The sacrament which takes up this aspect of the Christian life has fallen on hard times over recent decades. These hard times involve a much diminished use of the sacrament, and a frequently reported dissatisfaction with the experience of the sacrament on the part of both penitents and confessors. The life of the Church and of the individual Christian needs conversion to be authentic. The present malaise in which the sacrament of penance finds itself can act as a stimulus to our looking back through our history in order to rediscover the richness of our tradition and so to be able to move ahead.

In the first part of this book we will look back into our tradition as best we can with the help of theologians and historians. Among these historians we will enlist particularly the help of social historians whose study leads them to look at not just what the Church thought and proposed but what the Church was doing throughout its often turbulent history. This will lead us into an appreciation of what was actually being celebrated and practised in the many rituals and usages of the Church throughout its history. Such practices of the Church often do not quite fit later and neater theologies, yet these practices and the Church's concurrent understanding of them may be enlightening and helpful in meeting new situations.

In looking at the situation of the sacrament of penance today, its history is extremely important. No other sacrament has such a diverse history or has so many 'traditions' woven into it. No other sacrament has been so structurally and spiritually influenced by cultural change. In our current period of great cultural change, the past of the sacrament is enlightening, encouraging and enriching.

The second and more theological part of the book does not attempt anything like a complete presentation of *all* the themes involved in the sacrament of penance. However, in that part, I will concentrate on the foundations of this sacrament – and all the sacraments – in the Scriptures, the death and resurrection of Jesus, and the concept of memorial. In dealing with these foundational topics, and in the remaining chapters which follow their treatment, I will be particularly concerned to deal with those issues which seem to be crucial for our contemporary understanding of the sacrament and for our need to find fruitful forms for celebrating it.

As will become clear in the course of this book, the most important thing to achieve regarding this sacrament is a change of mentality. It is only with a changed mentality that we will be able to come to a fruitful renewal of it. It is my hope that this book may be a useful contribution to that achievement.

This book has come about because of the urging of my brother priests at a Convention of the Australian National Council of Priests. I thank them for their confidence and encouragement which led me to leave aside other projects to take up this one.

PART 1

The History of the Sacrament of Penance

Introduction

Over the last several decades we have come to see that the origin of each of the sacraments is more complex than we would once have imagined. It has become clear that the historical, cultural and religious situation of the early Church shaped the form each sacrament took and the understanding underlying each one. It has become clear too that changes in the Church's ongoing history have had considerable effects on the development of each sacrament. The sacraments have undergone the shaping influence of human culture and history within the life of the Church, while they have yet remained central to the Church's communication with Christ, its Lord.

Within this awareness of the complexity of the origins and development of the sacraments, the sacrament of penance stands out as having a particularly complex history. This is so because the sacrament, in the form in which we know it today, cannot be traced back to one single origin; rather, it goes back to diverse origins, one of which reaches back to the Church of the first century and even to Judaism, while another origin reaches back to fifth-century practices. Especially prominent among these practices were those of the Irish Church, which had its own particular institutions and customs. Yet a third tradition, which arose in the twelfth and thirteenth centuries, has come down to us in the twenty-first century.

I have entitled the first part of this book 'The History of the Sacrament of Penance'. But while this is an adequate title from our contemporary point of view, we must be aware that such a title has a somewhat different meaning to Catholic ears after the thirteenth century from the one it would have had before that time. In the patristic and early medieval Church, the word 'sacrament' had a much broader meaning, taking in many activities and actions of the Church, some of which later theology would describe as 'sacraments' and others as 'sacramentals'. In that earlier time, such rituals as blessing with holy water, the seasons of the liturgical year, the Creed and the kiss of peace were described as sacraments. Among all of these 'sacraments', Eucharist and baptism were seen to stand out as particularly significant.

Gradually theologians and canonists began to make lists of sacraments in a more specific sense. In the twelfth century, a standard list of seven sacraments came to be accepted. It was the theologian, Peter Lombard, whose listing came to be accepted. His works were the standard 'textbook' of the theological schools of the thirteenth century and so were very influential.

For our purposes, this means that speaking about the sacrament of penance when dealing with the period up to the twelfth century is rather anachronistic and can quite easily distort our thinking. The Church in that earlier period did not understand or practise rituals of penance with all the significance that the later Church would read into the word 'sacrament'. In that earlier period, the Church had what we might call 'penitential rituals' or 'penitential institutions'. It had in fact quite a range of such rites, as witnessed to in the New Testament, the writings of the Fathers of the Church and in those of later theologians and historians. Such practices included confession to each other, fraternal correction, prayers of confession, fasting, almsgiving, prayer, and, particularly, the praying of the Lord's Prayer.

Along with these practices, which formed part of the general life of the Church and which were used in reference to the constant and daily sinfulness of the members of the

Church, there were also more dramatic forms of penance used for more serious sins. These practices stand in a line of continuity with what we refer to today as the sacrament of penance.

We are about to enter into a long consideration of the history of the sacrament of penance which will comprise the first five chapters of this book. This will indeed enable us to see into the origins of our recent practice, but hopefully it will also enable us to have a grasp of the great riches of our tradition concerning all that is involved in the sacrament of penance and to see that recent centuries have formed and shaped that tradition in a particular way. The direction which recent centuries have given that tradition is indeed particular and has been determined by the needs, circumstances and culture – religious and general – of those centuries.

Thus the historical section of this book is very important in that it enables us to see that the Church has approached the related matters of forgiveness, conversion and sin in different, though related, ways and has had a wider range of strategies in dealing with them than only those we have known in recent centuries.

The history of the Church's institutions of penance will also alert us to the fact that there is a strong correlation between these institutions and the circumstances and cultures of the times in which they arose and were used. We will see that this was true of canonical penance and the Church of the first four centuries, of Irish penance and the Church of the early Middle Ages, and of 'confession' and the twelfth/ thirteenth century period in which it arose. Such correlations have to make us ask questions about our own practice of penance and the age of cultural transition in which we live. It is not enough just to state this, however: we need to see something of those historical correlations in the next few chapters in order for them to act as models to move us on.

There can be a temptation to try to reduce these diverse practices of the Church to one another, to attempt to show that they are just modifications of each other. The historical solidity of these various practices will not allow us to do this, as we will see. They are quite firmly different. We can of course recognise the elements they have in common, as well as those in which they differ.

Chapter 1

The First Tradition: Penance of Exclusion and Reconciliation

The first tradition which lies at the origins of the sacrament of penance originated in the churches around the Mediterranean Basin, where the Church first came into existence. It is sometimes referred to as 'Mediterranean penance'.[1]

The form taken by penance in this tradition was that of exclusion from the community. It was imposed on a member of the community because of sin so serious that it threatened the identity and well-being of the community itself. The offence was seen as contradictory to the perpetrator's belonging to the community and so as a betrayal of it. Such sin was seen to have the capacity to be destructive to the community, thus requiring drastic redressive action. In 1 Corinthians 5:1-13, where Paul is instructing the Corinthians about what to do with a man who committed incest, he says that he must be 'handed over to Satan', that is, to the destructive power which the sinner has manifested in his action. 'Handing over to Satan' does not imply that there was never to be forgiveness for the sinner. Rather, Paul says: 'hand such a man over to Satan, to be destroyed as far as natural life is concerned so that on the Day of the Lord his spirit may be saved' (v. 5). This procedure of exclusion was about making clear what the Church is and means; it was essentially an ecclesial action. We could compare the sort of offences that required this form of penance in the ancient Church to the sexual abuse of children by clergy in today's Church. Such offences called the Church's identity into question and threatened the well-being of the community in the way that such abuse does today.

This practice was an exercise of the power of 'binding and loosing' mentioned in Matthew's Gospel (16:19; 18:18) and that of 'forgiving and retaining' mentioned in John's (20:22-23). The term 'binding and loosing' is a technical Rabbinic term which involves the authority to make decisions which have consequences in the community. The practice of exclusion was an exercise of that power but it did not exhaust it.[2] The power of 'forgiving and retaining' in John's Gospel speaks of the same authority given by Jesus to his disciples after the Resurrection. This power in John is 'the power to isolate, repel and negate evil and sin, a power given to Jesus in his mission by the Father and given in turn by Jesus through the Spirit to those whom he commissions'.[3] We cannot simply identify the practice of exclusion penance with this power 'to bind and loose' or 'to forgive and retain' but it was an exercise of that power in the apostolic Church.

The practice of exclusion has its origins in a Jewish practice. The Church took over this practice – along with so much else – from the life of the Jewish people. The Jewish practice was called the 'ban'. It deprived the person who was put under it of their status as an Israelite but it could be restored to them if they gave up what caused the ban to be imposed. The ban was imposed on tax collectors, for instance, because they were collaborators with the Romans and so were not regarded as true Israelites. The ban could be imposed temporarily, which was known as the 'little ban', or permanently, known as the 'great ban'. The great ban was imposed after two failures of the little ban.

There are interesting parallels between the later order of penitents, and the older practices involved in putting people under the ban. The latter could not cut their hair, bathe or exchange greetings and could be part of Jewish worship only at a distance. As we will see, there are striking parallels between such practices and those of Christian exclusion penance.[4]

We have little evidence of the details of the practices of first and early second century churches in their use of exclusion from the community. It seems that some churches were more rigorous than others in dealing with sinners, but our documents give us only passing glimpses of this stage of the practice.[5]

Such a practice of exclusion from the group is not just a Jewish and Christian practice but is found in many cultures and religious traditions as a way of dealing with those whose behaviour is seen as destructive to the group or society to which they belong. In fact the same principle of the exclusion of the sinner from the community exists in our contemporary imprisonment of criminals. The exclusion is even more radical in the use of the death penalty!

We can begin to trace the development of this form of penance in the period beyond the New Testament with a document written between 100 and 150 in Rome called *The Shepherd of Hermas*.[6]

The background to the issues of sin and repentance as they are dealt with in this document seems to have been dissension in the Church about whether those who had sinned seriously should be permitted to be members of it again after repenting of their sin or whether they should be permanently excluded. There seems to have been a rigorist opinion abroad which held that there was only one penance, which was baptism, with its catechumenal process of which conversion was the essential element. A Christian who sinned after baptism was to be permanently excluded from the Church. This view was based on a strong sense of the holiness of the Church – so strong, in fact, that post-baptismal sin was seen as a complete and irreparable betrayal.

The Shepherd of Hermas takes a different position from the rigorists. *The Shepherd* proposes that there should be the possibility of penance after baptism; however, this should be allowed only once. Those who had sinned seriously could go through a process of readmission to the Church parallel to the process of 'penance' involved in baptism. This position held a middle line on the questions of the seriousness of sin and of compassion for the sinner. The fact that post-baptismal penance was allowed was compassionate and yet the once-only nature of this penance guarded against a loosening of the sense of the seriousness of sin.

The Shepherd came to be held in very high esteem in the ancient Church. It circulated very widely. In some lists it was counted with the writings of the New Testament. Its position on penance became the position of the Church all over the Mediterranean world; that is, post-baptismal penance was to be allowed, but once only. This position became a 'quasi–dogma' of the Church.[7] It was the parallel with baptism which gave this position such strength. Just as there could be only one baptism, so there could be only one penance, and just as there would be an order of catechumens going through a process of conversion towards baptism and Eucharist, so there would be an order of penitents going through a process of conversion towards reconciliation achieved in re-admittance to Eucharist. This also accounts for the name which emerged for post-baptismal penance – *penitentia secunda* (second penance) – over against baptism, which was *penitentia prima* (first penance).

The underside to this position, as we shall see, is that what began as a practice based on compassion would become itself a form of rigorism in the later history of penance: the once-only nature of penance would come to prevent its effective use.

Third century controversies

We begin to catch more detailed glimpses of 'second penance' in the third century and we catch these glimpses largely because of controversies occurring in the life of the Church.

Tertullian

The first of these controversies involves Tertullian, the first theologian to write in Latin. He was born in Carthage in North Africa around 160 and was converted to Christianity about 190. He began his theological writing around 197. His first writings were Catholic in doctrine but by 213 he was attracted to the heresy of Montanism and left the Catholic Church to join the Montanist sect. It was his attraction to Montanism which led to his disagreement with the Church's discipline of the *penitentia secunda*.

Montanus had been a converted pagan priest who preached the coming end of the world and therefore the need for repentance. He eventually claimed that he himself was the Holy Spirit who had come to complete the revelation of Christ. This claim soon led to the separation of this group from the Church. According to Montanus, the Church can forgive any sin but ought not to because such forgiveness would encourage sin. There were rigorists throughout the Church who sympathised with this position. Montanus' influence forced the issue and the Church had to reassert the position of reconciling sinners which had by that time developed as the Church's formal position.

Tertullian's own position on penance changed after he joined the Montanists. In the *Tractatus de Penitentia* of his Catholic period he held that forgiveness and reconciliation were possible for all sinners but only once and so he agreed with the official position of the Catholic Church. In his later *De pudicitia* he speaks against what he sees at that time as the indulgent position of the Catholic bishops and maintains the rigorist position that penance and reconciliation should not be given at all after baptism.

A generation later in the same third century, we see the rise of two other controversies about penance, and both of them concern the continuing presence of rigorism in the Church. These two controversies – one in Rome and the other in North Africa – are separated geographically but are related ecclesially and theologically.

During the late second and third centuries the membership of the Church increased considerably. The estimated number of Christians in the Roman Empire by the end of the third century was one tenth of the population. It would have been the biggest single distinctive religious group in the Empire, though its numbers would have been greater in the eastern provinces of the Empire than in its western provinces.[8] Likewise we know that around the middle of the third century, when the controversies with which we are concerned were current, there were forty-six presbyters and over one hundred other official ministers in the Church of the City of Rome. Thus we are no longer dealing with very small communities of people, as was the case in the earlier part of the second century. And, of course, social dynamics change as the size of a group changes.

Cyprian and North Africa

What gave rise to this controversy and its parallel controversy in Rome was the persecution initiated by Emperor Decius in 250. This persecution was both widespread and vicious, and the Church was unprepared for it as it came after a long period of freedom from persecution. Many Christians were unable to persevere during this persecution and apostasised by offering worship to the gods. These Christians were called *lapsi* ('the fallen'). Yet some other Christians were able to obtain *libelli* (certificates) which stated that they had offered worship to the gods even though they had not. They obtained these through the good offices of friends or for a 'consideration'.

Once the persecution was over, the Church was faced with the issue of what to do with the considerable number of *lapsi*. The rigorists wanted to refuse them re-entry into the Church. There were also those at the other end of the spectrum who would have re-admitted them immediately, especially if they obtained recommendations from any of those who had suffered during the persecutions. These latter were called 'confessors' – not in the later meaning of the word associated with the sacrament of penance but meaning those who had continued to confess their faith even under torture.

Cyprian and the bishops of North Africa decided in synod that those who had merely obtained certificates to say they had sacrificed, but had not in fact sacrificed, would be reconciled immediately, but that those who had actually sacrificed to the gods or had offered incense to the emperor's image would be reconciled after a determined period of penance. Cyprian warned against too quick a reconciliation which might underestimate the gravity of what they had done and not allow sufficient time for genuine repentance. Some months later there was a threat of further persecution, in response to which it was decided that all penitents should be reconciled.

Pope Cornelius in Rome

In the course of these controversies in Carthage, letters were sent from Carthage to Rome to consult the Roman Church on its policy in regard to the treatment of the *lapsi* who sought reconciliation with the Church. At that moment there happened to be no bishop in Rome. The election of a new bishop had been impeded by the Decian persecution. Novatian, the secretary of the Roman Presbyterium during the interregnum sent replies to Cyprian which accorded with Cyprian's policy of reconciliation after a suitable period of penance. Significantly, in view of what was to follow, there was considerable contrast in the tone of the letters; Cyprian's letters showed compassion for those who had fallen, while the tone of the Roman letters was harsh.

After the election of a new Bishop of Rome, Pope Cornelius, the Roman policy of reconciliation of the *lapsi* after a period of penance was reaffirmed. In response to this,

Novatian set up a rival Church with himself as bishop. In this Novatian Church, reconciliation was refused to those who had fallen away. A Roman synod convoked by Pope Cornelius excommunicated Novatian and his followers. A rigorist Novatian Church continued to exist for some time in Gaul and even in the eastern parts of the Roman Empire.

Penitential process in the third century

We do not have a lot of detail concerning the actual process of penance in the third century. We know it that was modelled on the baptismal process of the catechumenate since it was conceived as a re-tracing of the baptismal process and, like baptism, could be received only once. This link to baptism also meant that the penitents formed a group within the Church doing penance and preparing for reconciliation in parallel to the group of catechumens preparing for baptism. This group was known as the 'order of penitents'; they were alongside other orders making up the community of the Church, for example, the order of catechumens, the order of the faithful and the order of presbyters.

There were two ritual moments in the penitential process: that of entry into penance and that of the reconciliation of the penitents. We know little of the form of 'entry into penance' for this period; the 'reconciliation of sinners' mainly involved the return of the penitents to the celebration of the community's Eucharist.

Second, or post-baptismal, penance was used only for grave sin: idolatry, adultery and murder were the three sins typically requiring it. The activities required to be done during the period of penance consisted of various measures of the three classical acts of devotion and penance: prayer, fasting and almsgiving. These were also part of the catechumenal process. The penitents were prayed over frequently and received the laying on of hands from the bishop.

The fourth and fifth centuries

In the fourth and fifth centuries we find the Fathers of the Church writing about three types of penance: pre-baptismal penance; post-baptismal, or canonical, penance; and penance for daily sins. The pre-baptismal penance was that of the catechumenate, the post-baptismal was for serious sin after baptism, and the daily penance was for the daily sins of the faithful. This last form of penance involved all that forms part of the Christian life: prayer, fasting, and charity, in the broadest sense of these words. St Augustine spoke of praying the Lord's Prayer as a way in which our daily sins are forgiven.[9]

During the second and third centuries, as we have seen, the form of post-baptismal penance developed gradually, with differences according to place and circumstances. In the fourth century, post-baptismal penance became more organised. This organisation was laid down by canons (directives or laws) of various councils. In this period we can properly call it 'canonical penance'.

Canonical penance involved three stages which, together, were an elaboration of the basic form of post-baptismal penance which had developed in the third century. The whole penitential process took place publicly as part of the life of the Christian community. The penitents were a segregated group within that community from whose eucharistic communion they were excluded. The process had three parts: entry into penance, the period for doing penance and the reconciliation of the penitents with the Church.

The first stage – entrance into penance – was the penitents' formal, ritual exclusion from the community to a life on its edge in the order of penitents. At least in some instances they were sprinkled with ashes and clothed in sackcloth as part of the ritual.

The second stage – the period of penance itself – involved a considerable length of time, the duration of which was determined either by the bishop or, increasingly, as time went on, by the canons of various synods. The penitents were to be constant in prayer and were regularly prayed over by the bishop and the gathered faithful. They were expected to fast strictly and to give alms. There were particular signs of their status, such as being shaved or, alternatively, having to let their hair grow; they were not to be concerned with cleanliness; certain professions were forbidden to them: service in the army, being a merchant, taking public office, ordination in the Church; and conjugal relations were forbidden. In many places, these prohibitions regarding occupation and conjugal relations lasted for the rest of their lives, even after they had been reconciled with the Church. In such cases they were effectively penitents for the rest of their lives.

The final stage of canonical penance – the reconciliation of the penitents – took place in the full liturgical assembly of the people around the bishop. Their reconciliation was their re-admission to the Eucharist by the bishop. This was preceded by the laying on of hands with a prayer of reconciliation. In Rome from the fifth century on, this reconciliation took place on Holy Thursday.

It is noteworthy that this process became stricter and more structured in the period after Constantine's recognition of, and favour towards, the Church, that is, in a period when more and more people were becoming Christians, and they were doing so without the benefit of the thorough catechumenate which had existed in the second and third centuries.

Canonical penance was available only once and only for the laity; the clergy were left 'to the mercy of God'.

Exceptions to the full use of canonical penance were declared when Christians came to be in danger of death.

In that situation, they were to be reconciled immediately. If, however, reconciled former penitents subsequently recovered from their illness, they were expected to 'do penance', that is, to enter the order of penitents and to go through the whole process required of any other penitent.

The system of canonical penance could not fulfil its purpose. By the mid fifth century, it fell into disuse under the weight of its own severity, its once-only character, and its often lifelong restrictions. It was simply impractical for ordinary people living normal lives in the world. One author points out that it was insupportable for normal healthy Christians.[10] This impracticality was canonically recognised, that is, in the very canons or regulations of bishops gathered in synods.[11] They recommended that it was not to be used by anyone young, even by young married people.[12] The leaders of the Church were well aware that this system could not be used effectively and yet, for the most part, they had no alternative to offer. In fact, even when an alternative did appear, many of the bishops were so convinced that the ancient canons had to be adhered to that they denied the validity of the new system emerging in Europe under the influence of the Irish monks.[13]

Thus the only way in which reconciliation was available to most Christians at this time was as deathbed penance. Christians tended to keep their once-only opportunity for penance after baptism until they were close to their death. Penance virtually became the sacrament of the dying.

The whole ritual of penance was used with dying persons. They went through the rite of entry into penance, the prayers and laying on of hands at the time of penance and the rite of reconciliation of penitents. So whatever rites were used by the various particular churches for the whole penitential process were telescoped and used with the dying. This meant that the rites of penance in their most commonly used form came to be separated from the process of interior conversion in which they were originally embedded and which had given them their specific meaning.

St Caesarius of Arles

St Caesarius of Arles (470–542) bears witness to the demise of canonical penance among the faithful while seeking to give new meaning to its use as deathbed penance. He inherited a pastoral situation in which Christians were delaying the use of canonical penance until the time of their death because of the impracticality discussed above.

Yet, there were other Church leaders contemporary with Caesarius who saw no value at all in deathbed penance. The awareness that such rigorist opinions were in circulation created anxiety in Caesarius' congregation, and he admits in his sermons that heated discussion on the matter had generated considerable animosity.

The unease about whether penance received at death was effective led Caesarius to spend a considerable proportion of his preaching time dealing with the issue. He warned that deathbed penance was not absolute and unconditional but depended upon serious preparation and that such preparation depended upon living a life of serious conversion expressed in prayer and good works. For Caesarius everything depended upon the disposition of the penitent.

Although he still saw public canonical penance as the only remedy for serious sin, he accepted the fact that this would happen only at the time of death for virtually all the members of his congregation. In effect his preaching reversed the order of the process of penance in that he urged Christians to live now the life of conversion which would make deathbed penance effective at the time of death.[14]

An interesting side issue concerns the practice of canonical penance. Entry into monastic life or life as a *conversus* was seen as an alternative to penance. (*Conversi* were persons who, although they did not enter a monastery, formally dedicated their lives to prayer, fasting and self-denial). It was because these two forms of life – monastic life and the life of a *conversus* – involved the elements that made up the period of penance in canonical penance, they were considered the equivalent of entry into penance and so anyone taking on either of these came to be considered reconciled to God and the Church by their very state of life.[15]

The thought and practice of St Caesarius is a good point at which to conclude our description of the first tradition of penitential practice in the history of the Church. As he presents it to us, it had ceased to function in accord with the original intention behind its institution.

The order of penitents

There are however important reflections to be made on the first tradition of penitential practice in order to appreciate the nature of the sacrament of penance in the life of the Church. In the organisation of canonical penance, the penitents were gathered into their own *ordo*, or rank, in the life and structure of the Church. The order of penitents paralleled the order of catechumens, the order of the faithful, the order of deacons, the order of presbyters and so on. This is a significant point because it indicates the truly ecclesial nature of the process of penance, that is, that it belongs to the Church by its nature. Each of the above orders has their own role to play in the Church and each of them expresses a particular dimension or aspect of the Church: each of them symbolises some aspect of the overall mystery of the Church in its relationship with Christ.

Awareness of the ecclesial nature of penance was significant in the disputes over the admission or rejection of sinners into the Church after serious sin: in these disputes Church leaders were not just dealing with a question of compassion but a question of the Church's nature. It was a matter of the Church coming to grips with itself as made up of human beings marked by sin as well as by the holiness which comes from Christ. The Church was not to be seen as a purist sect. This in turn involved avoiding the illusion of perfection. In having an order of penitents the Church symbolised what it is in itself – holy yet sinful – rather than pretending that sin could be excluded from its life and members, as implied in the position of the rigorist sects.

The penitents had their own place within the assembly of the Church and in the building in which that assembly took place. They were marked out by different clothing, posture and physical location within the assembly. They begged the prayers of the faithful as they gathered to celebrate the Eucharist in which they themselves could not participate. Such penitents embodied the *Ecclesia paenitens*, the Church penitent, the Church seeking conversion.

To make the same point: in many of the later rituals for public penance contained in our sources, the bishop began the process of the penitents' exclusion, or entry into penance, with the recognition of his own sinfulness.[16] Similarly, the interplay of the penitents and the faithful in the rites showed a liturgical identification between them, coupled with an expression of the difference between the two groups.[17]

Context

It is important to put this system of penance into its proper context, though there are two contexts within which I would like to situate it.

The first context is that of a particular sociological form of the Church which can be described as sect-like. Canonical penance of exclusion originated when the Church had the form of a small tightly knit community which was either disregarded by, or lived under threat from, the surrounding society. It was, sociologically speaking, a sect, even if theologically it was not, as would be revealed later. But being sociologically a sect, its behaviour was sect-like and needed to be so. It therefore protected itself and its identity from outside influences. It took much time and care in initiating new members (catechumenate); it had a discipline of the secret by which it protected its rituals and sacred objects from the eyes and ears of those outside the group; and its procedure for re-introducing members who had fallen away was in line with those of other sect-like groups.

Once the Christian communities became better known, recognised and tolerated and included larger numbers of the citizens of the wider community, the sect-like character of the Church began to disappear and, sociologically, as well as theologically, it became a 'Church', that is, a group made up of citizens of their surrounding society largely sharing the culture of that society. To the extent that the Church ceased to be a sect, the exclusion system of penance began to falter, and, indeed, to cease to function at all because it was a structure which belonged to an earlier stage of the Church's socio-structural development.

We can see parallels to that early social structure of the Church in the nineteenth and twentieth centuries: situations in which the Church was a subculture, as was the case in some Anglo-Saxon countries, or in which the Church was under threat from the surrounding society, as was the case in communist countries. In such situations, the Church firms up its boundaries and has strict regulations about such things as marrying outside the Church (i.e., beyond the boundaries). Insistence on rituals which re-enforce identity (e.g., not eating meat on Fridays, everyone being at Mass on Sundays) becomes a means of protecting and nourishing the group. Such practices will function effectively because of the broader social situation but they will not function so effectively once the Church's relationship to the surrounding society becomes one of a shared culture. From this point of view, the canonical system of penance of exclusion was doomed once the Church became accepted within, and began to share, the culture of the surrounding society. It is to this collapse of canonical penance in a new social situation that witnesses like Caesarius of Arles testify.

The second context in which we must locate the practice of canonical penance relates to the existence of similar structures of exclusion in other societies. The studies of anthropologists have led us to see that structures of exclusion like that involved in canonical penance are not specifically Christian but comprise one specific type of structure used in societies all over the world to deal with those who cannot be contained or tolerated by their society because their actions are socially destructive. Many strategies for dealing with such individuals have been devised: capital punishment, exile, imprisonment, bodily incapacitation and so on. The form of exclusion used by the ancient Church was one among these possibilities. The choice of one form over other forms depends upon the circumstances, values and possibilities of the group. Such a choice reveals something about the nature of the group. For this reason it was important that the dissension between various Catholic leaders and the rigorists was resolved in the way it was. It was revealing the nature of the Church.

The cultural dimension of this penitential structure must be recognised if we are to evaluate it. It is by bringing into view the use of this structure in human societies that we are able to ascertain the reasons for its eventual loss of effectiveness. This was not a ritual peculiar to the Church which had been specifically ordained by God in its actual structures but it was a structure which the Church found in the human world in which it lived and which it used to express the Christian realities of conversion and reconciliation. It was an effective social structure in a certain situation but it did not function effectively outside that context.

Recognising these anthropological structures enables us to explain how Cyprian and Cornelius were correct in their resolution of the mid third century problems with the rigorists and to explain the frustration of a Caesarius of Arles caught between the established penitential system of canonical penance, on the one hand, and, on the other, the struggles of his people trying to be good Christians in a difficult and anxious age while being left without the ritual assurance of God's forgiveness that they needed. The Church was not in its living reality what the penitential system symbolically said it was.

A consequence

In the fourth century, many people became Christians by becoming catechumens and remained so until close to the time of their deaths. In this way they were of the household of the faith, yet, by delaying their baptisms until the end of their lives, they did not have to take on the full seriousness of being a Christian. This also meant that they did not receive Communion at the Eucharist.

The penitential system was a part of their reason for taking the option of delayed baptism since it could be administered only once and many of them were well aware of their fragility. So, with a combination of catechumens delaying baptism until near the end of their lives and baptised Christians in need of penance but delaying that penance to the end of their lives, the number of people communicating at the Eucharist diminished. There arose a largely non-communicating Church throughout most of the centuries of the Middle Ages.

The structure of penance – initially instituted to be used once only as a measure of compassion in the writings of the Shepherd of Hermas – came to reinforce a rigorist position. The very structure of the penitential process was the problem: it was so tied to an earlier stage of the Church's life which came to be identified with the rigorist position that it was unable to express the compassion for which it had been designed.

Notes

1. John Dallen, *The Reconciling Community* (New York: Pueblo Publishing Company, 1986) 7-12, 19-21; Joseph A. Favazza, *The Order of Penitents: Historical roots and pastoral future* (Collegeville: The Liturgical Press, 1988) 71, 72, 76-7, 81-2; Philippe Rouillard, *Histoire de la pénitence des origines à nos jours* (Paris: Cerf, 1996) 27-42; Cyrille Vogel, *Le pécheur et la pénitence dans l'église ancienne* (Paris: Cerf, 1966); Louis–Marie Chauvet, ' "Nova et Vetera": quelques leçons tirées de la tradition relative au sacrement de la réconciliation', in P. De Clerk and E. Palazzo, dir., *Rituels: Mélanges offerts au Père Gy OP* (Paris: Cerf, 1993) 99-124.

2. Daniel J. Harrington, *The Gospel of Matthew*. Sacra Pagina 1 (Collegeville: The Liturgical Press. A Michael Glazier Book, 1991) 246-52 and 268-72.

3. Raymond Brown, *The Gospel According to John, XIII–XXI*. The Anchor Bible (London: Geoffrey Chapman, 1971) 1044-5; Francis J. Moloney, *The Gospel of John*. Sacra Pagina 4 (Collegeville: The Liturgical Press: A Michael Glazier Book, 1998) 529-36.

4. G. Forkman, *The Limits of Religious Community: Expulsion from the religious community within the Qumran sect, within rabbinic Judaism and within primitive Christianity*. Coniectanea Biblica, NT Series 5 (Lund, Sweden: GWK Gleerup, 1972).

5. Commentators suggest that the following New Testament texts may show signs of rigorism: 1 John 5:14-17, Heb 6:4-8, 10:26-31, 12:16-17. The New Testament by and large is unambiguous about God's mercy for the sinner. This is shown in such highly significant texts as Matt 18:12–35 and Luke 15.

6. This document can be found in collections of the writings of the Apostolic Fathers, e.g., in Jack Sparks, ed., *The Apostolic Fathers* (Nashville/New York: Thomas Nelson Inc. Publishers, 1978) 155-259.

7. Louis-Marie Chauvet, 'Évolutions et révolutions du sacrement de la réconciliation', in Louis-Marie Chauvet and Paul De Clerck, dir., *Le sacrement du pardon entre hier et domain* (Paris: Desclée, 1993) 35-7.

8. For these details, see Wolfgang Wischmeyer, 'The Sociology of Pre–Constantine Christianity: Approach from the visible', in Alan Kreider, ed., *The Origins of Christendom in the West* (Edinburgh/New York: T. and T. Clark, 2001) 129.

9. M.-F. Berrouard, 'Pénitence de tous les jours selon saint Augustin', *Lumiere et Vie* Tome 13, no. 70 (1964) 51-74. For Augustine's text, see his *Sermo 352*, Patrologia Latina 39, 1549-60.

10. M.–F. Berrouard, 'Le pénitence publique durant les six premiers siecles: histoire et sociologie'. *Maison Dieu* 118 (1974) 128.

11. ibid., 128; Vogel, *Le pécheur*, 39-40.

12. Berrouard, *Le pénitence publique*, 126; Vogel, *Le pécheur*, 39-40; C. Munier, 'La pastorale pénitentielle de saint Cesaire d'Arles (503-543)', *Revue de Droit Canonique* 34 (1984) 239.

13. Cyrille Vogel, *Il peccatore e la penitenza nel medioevo* (Leumann [Torino]: Editrice Elle Di Ci, 1970) 14–5.

14. Munier, *La pastorale pénitentielle*, 235–44; Cyrille Vogel, 'La paenitentia in extremis chez saint Césaire évêque d'Arles', *Studia Patristica* 5 (1962) 416-32; Cyrille Vogel, *Césaire d'Arles* (Paris: Bloud et Anè, 1964).

15. Vogel, *Le pécheur*, 49-50.

16. Mary Mansfield, *The Humiliation of Sinners: Public penance in thirteenth century France* (Ithaca/ London: Cornell University Press, 1995) 37-8; François Bussini, 'L'intervention de l'évêque dans la réconciliation des pénitents d'après les trois 'postulations' d'un archidiacre romain du Ve-Vie siècle', *Revue des Sciences Religiueses* 42 (1968) 326-38.

17. François Bussini, 'L'intervention de l'assemblée des fedeles au moment de la réconciliation des penitents d'après les trois 'postulations' d'un archidiacre romain di Ve-VIe siècle', *Revue des Sciences Religieuses* 41 (1967) 29-38.

Chapter 2

The Second Tradition: Tariff Penance

Having looked at the first tradition in the history of the Church's dealing with sin and penance, we come now to look at the second. This second line of development arose in Ireland in the late fifth or early sixth centuries. Patrick had returned to Ireland to begin his missionary activity in 452, the year after the gathering of bishops for the Council of Chalcedon. By the late sixth century, the great Irish missionaries were moving into Britain and onto the continent of Europe to evangelise or re-evangelise those lands. With these Irish missionaries came a new form of penance, called 'tariff penance', which had come to birth in the Irish Church.

Between Patrick's arrival and the seventh century, the Irish Church developed in a unique way. Instead of diocesan structures based on a bishop with his see centred in a city, which was the structure that had developed within the Europe of the Roman Empire, there developed in Ireland a monastic structure which determined the government, spirituality and customs of the Church. Just as the European structure showed the influence of the governmental structures of the Roman Empire, so the structures of the Irish Church showed the influence of the structures by which Ireland lived and was governed. The Roman Empire was an empire based on cities; Ireland, on the other hand, was a rural and tribal society based on a large number of petty kingdoms linked to the kings of the provinces who, in turn, were linked to the High King in his capital of Tara.[1]

The monasteries of Ireland took on the form of these petty kingdoms and functioned according to parallel structures. As the historian, Patrick Geary, says: '... in the sixth century, the Irish Church became a federation of monastic communities corresponding roughly to a tribe and each under the jurisdiction of the heir of the founding saint of the region'.[2]

These monasteries were much more complex organisations than we may imagine. They were made up of a considerable variety of people: monks and nuns, in the strict sense of these terms, other clerics, scholars studying at the monastery, penitents and lay tenants of the monastery. All of these were under the authority of the abbot who had not only religious but also civil jurisdiction over them. These were societies in which the separation of the religious and the civil was inconceivable.

These monasteries would seem to have been the matrix from which the tariff form of penance emerged. The authorship of the 'Penitentials', or Penitential Books, which were the basis of this tariff penance, were attributed to some of the most significant figures of the Irish Church, and the particular character of this form of penance makes sense when it is seen in terms of its monastic origins and setting.

The form of penance envisaged in tariff penance did not have the strictly ecclesial and liturgical structures which we saw in the exclusion form of penance. It had a more individual character in which a sinner approached a monk and acknowledged his or her sins. The penitent was then given works of penance to do as the means of dealing with those sins and of bringing about conversion. This form had echoes of spiritual direction to it, one of the basic activities of monastic life.

This form of penance dealt with sins of considerable gravity and sins which, at least at times, might also be expected to carry a civil punishment with them. Each type of sin was given an appropriate tariff and that tariff was set out in the Penitential Book. It was not up to the confessor to decide on the penance; the penance which was set down in the Book had to be applied. The principle of compensation was at work in this form of penance and in this it showed the influence of the Brehon laws of Ireland. They, like the Germanic systems of law on the Continent, were based on the *wergeld* principle, that is, on a system of set, specific compensations for specific offences.

It was this form of penance which was carried by the Irish monks into Europe and which they introduced to those people to whom they brought the Christian faith. The evidence we have for the presence of this penance comes particularly from those areas where Irish missionaries were to spread.

Tariff penance

Tariff penance was based on the imposition of particular penances for particular sins. It is not appropriately named 'confession', as later forms of penance would be, because the actual confession was only a precursor to the penitential activity. The purpose of naming the sin was to be able to calculate and quantify the amount of penance which needed to be done. The particular character of this form of penance was in 'doing penance'. It was in the fulfilling of that penance that the sins were forgiven.[3]

The acknowledgment of sin could be spontaneous or it could be according to a questionnaire administered by the confessor. The penance imposed consisted of various kinds of mortification in accord with the seriousness and number of the sins. These penances would consist of fasting, prayer, prolonged vigils, prostrations, gifts of money, ceasing of marital relations, pilgrimage and even exile. The fasts could be specific, that is, from various kinds of foods: wine, beer, meat, fats and they could be for various lengths of time: days, weeks, months or years.

All of this penance was calculated according to the tariffs set down in the particular Penitential being used by a confessor, which would belong to a particular family, or type, of Penitential. These differed in their tariffs from one type of Penitential to another.

This form of penance had advantages over the penance of exclusion in that it was applicable to all Christians, including bishops and priests. It could in theory, at least, be undertaken as often as necessary, it was conducted privately whenever the penitent desired and there were no continuing disabilities once the penance was completed.

The forgiveness of the sins committed was considered achieved in the completion of the penance. Once the penance given was completed, ipso facto the sins were forgiven. There is no mention in any of the early Penitentials of an absolution or of a returning to the monk or priest after the completion of the penance. After 950, we do have mention of the penitent's being formally reconciled by the confessor and we do begin to find mention of absolution being given after the imposition of penance but before its completion.[4] We see here the beginning of a change in the order of the elements of the process of doing penance: reconciliation of the penitent began to be given before the completion of the penance. This would have seemed very strange indeed to those involved in either canonical penance or the earlier forms of tariff penance for whom the fulfilment of the penance was the substance of the penitential process.

In these changes we are probably seeing the influence of the Carolingian reform of the eighth and ninth centuries. Part of this reform was the principle that penance necessarily involved priest-confessors rather than monk-confessors. One of the principles of the Carolingian reform in its attempt to create greater order was to concentrate more and more things in the hands of presbyters.

The Penitentials

At the core of this system of penance were the books called 'Penitentials'. Penitentials, as we saw above, were books containing lists of sins alongside which were the appropriate tariffs (penances) to be given for each sin. They enabled the confessor to compute the necessary penance for the sins to be expiated.

The extant copies of Penitentials that we have are divided into three families: the Irish, the Anglo-Saxon and the Frankish. The Anglo-Saxon and the Frankish are generally considered to have been based on the Irish. Cummean's Penitential is considered the classic of the Irish family. Those of Columban and Finnian were widely used throughout Europe. The Anglo-Saxon Penitentials are characterised by having ecclesiastical canons added to them and the Frankish by having an order of private penance attached to them; this gave them something of the character of a liturgical book as well.[5]

One of the difficulties that arose with this system of penance was that the variety and diversity of the Penitentials was such that it meant that the same sins were treated with different degrees of severity. This resulted in confusion and a loss of confidence in their value.

Commutations and redemptions

The tariff system of penance had problems at the practical level just as the canonical system had had. The penances given were hard and long and so for the relatively active sinner the penances could mount up to such an extent that it became impossible to complete them within a normal lifetime.

To give an example, in the Penitential of Theodore, dated at the end of the seventh century, the sin of fornication required four years' fasting, the desire to fornicate required forty days' fasting, murder required ten years' fasting and taking a false oath required eleven years' fasting.[6] Adding just one instance of each of these sins together, the total duration of fasting required as penance would be twenty-five years and forty days. Quite a penitential task!

Such impracticality promoted the rise of new strategies to make tariff penance more practicable; hence 'commutations' and 'redemptions'. These strategies meant that a longer penance could be commuted into a shorter, but more severe one. One year of fasting on bread and water might be commuted to three days of total fasting done twelve times, or it might be commuted to a large number of prostrations or genuflections, or to reciting the Psalter three times, accompanied by blows of the whip, or to spending the night in a tomb with a corpse! These penances still involved considerable severity, but they were at least practicable.

Another form of redemption of a penance involved having someone else do it for the penitent. This meant hiring someone or, in the case of the rich, having a serf do it. So in the Penitential of Egard, dated around 960, a rich man who had seven years' fasting to do would instead pay twelve men to fast in his place for three days each, then 120 men to fast for three days, seven times. Thus we have the seven years' fasting (i.e., 2556 days: [12 x 3 days] + [120 x 3 days x 7] = 2556.)[7] As time went on, further kinds of commutation or redemption became very popular: they could be made in the form of money payments, so, for instance, three years' fasting could be redeemed by six gold solidi, or they could be made by having Masses said, for instance, one year's fasting could be redeemed by having thirty Masses said.[8] These strategies make us smile! But they fitted more logically into the mentality of the day in which this system of penance functioned. Of this we will speak later.

Diversity over canonical and tariff penance

As tariff penance spread and took hold in Europe, strongly conflicting positions arose between those promoting it and those still promoting penance 'according to the ancient canons'. There were two stages to this controversy: one occurring in the sixth and seventh centuries and the other occurring in the ninth century. It was generally local synods which were taking up opposing stances.

The Council of Toledo in Spain, which met in 589, reaffirmed the old canons and condemned the new system. The bishops at the council stated:

> We have come to learn that in certain Spanish churches men do penance for their sins not in accord with canonical precedent but in a most offensive manner namely, as often as they are pleased to sin, so often they demand of the presbyter to be reconciled. Accordingly, to suppress so execrable a presumption, the holy Council commands that penances be assigned according to the form of the ancient canons. This means that he shall require of the one who repents of his deed, after he has been suspended from communion, firstly to recur frequently to the imposition of the hand among the rest of the penitents; and when the period of satisfaction is completed to the approval of the priest's judgment, let him restore him to communion. Those, however, who lapse into their former vices, whether they do so before the period of penance or after reconciliation, let them be condemned in accord with the severity of the earlier canons. (Canon 11)[9]

This is somewhat surprising because we would not have expected the Irish system to have reached Spain but the description of the system of penance condemned is certainly of the Irish type.

We get an opposing stance to that of the Council of Toledo some sixty years later, between 644 and 656, at the Council at Chalons-sur-Soane, in Northern France. There, the bishops made the following statement:

> With regard to doing penance for sins ... we believe that this is valuable for all people, as well as this, it is the unanimous agreement of the bishops gathered in this assembly that,

after having made their confession, penitents should be given penance by the priests.[10]

The second stage of the controversy about tariff penance occurred at the time of the Carolingian reform, in the ninth century. The aim of this reform was to reinstate the use of canonical penance for those sins to which it had applied. Penitential Books, being central to tariff penance, were burnt. In 813, many local councils throughout Northern Gaul proposed a return to canonical penance. A Council at Chalons-sur-Saone in that year made a very different statement from the one made in that same city 150 years earlier:

> In many places the doing of penance according to the ancient institutions of the canons has lapsed from use, and nor is the order of the ancient custom of reconciliation observed: let help be sought from the lord emperor, that if anyone sins publicly he may be punished by public penance and be excommunicated and reconciled in accordance with his deserts according to the ancient canons. (Canon 25)
>
> Moreover the measure of penance to those who confess their sins ought to be imposed, as was said above, either by the institution of the ancient canons, or by the authority of the Holy Scriptures, or by ecclesiastical custom, the booklets which they call 'penitentials' being repudiated and utterly cast out, of which the errors are obvious, the authors undetermined, of which it might be fitly said: They slew souls which should not have died and saved souls alive which should not have lived … (Canon 38)[11]

A Council in Paris in 829 strongly attacked the books 'called Penitentials' and insisted on their being burnt:

> That the booklets which they call 'penitentials' be wholly abolished since they are opposed to the authority of the canons. Since many priests, partly due to carelessness and partly due to ignorance, impose the measure of penance on those who confess their state of sin at variance with what the canonical laws decree making use, forsooth, of certain booklets written in opposition to canonical authority, which

they call 'penitentials' and on this account, they do not cure the wounds of sinners, but rather bathe and stroke them ... to all of us in common it seemed salutary that each one of the bishops in his diocese diligently seek out these erroneous booklets and when they are found give them to the flames, that through them unskilled priests may no longer deceive men ... (Canon 32)[12]

These attempts to be rid of the new system of tariff penance proved unsuccessful. We shall see later that the effect of the Carolingian reform was to bring about a compromise.

The context of tariff penance

Tariff penance arose in a society which was different from that in which canonical penance arose. It was no longer the ecclesial world of the penance of exclusion. No longer was the Church formed by the catechumenate and living in sect-like social conditions: it was in a world in the birth pangs of Christendom, where Christianity and European society are coterminous. It was still a mixed world but the thrust was towards the identification of the society of the time with Christianity. In this way the institutions, laws and customs of societies were progressively Christianised in order that those being socialised into them would breathe in the air of Christianity and so become themselves Christians as individuals within their society. Evangelisation came to replace the catechumenate. By its means everyone would gradually become Christian by belonging to a Christian society.

In this context, the Church no longer sought to establish, nourish and guard its own identity within a broader society which was either unaware of it or inimical to it, but the Church sought to promote its own identity in all the individuals making up society. It was concerned to convert people by proclaiming the gospel and by bringing about in them the corresponding conversion required by the gospel. It was indeed a new culture and a new religious world coming into being. Not only was the Church's relationship to the overall society and its members different but the mentality within which these people lived and their religiosity were very different.

I am not suggesting that people formulated all of this explicitly; rather, they made pastoral-theological decisions as best they could in their situation. This was not simply a strategy formulated by an elite of Christians; it was a dialogue between the Church and the gospel and the mentality of the time. This dialogue was going on within those very believers themselves. They shared the mentality of those to whom they preached and with whom they made up the Church. There are elements in this mentality which we find strange and which we can be tempted to dismiss. We must, however, see those elements within their own proper cultural setting.

An example will illustrate the dialogue that had to occur between the gospel and the mentality of the time. The Christian version of human life involves the recognition of sin, repentance and forgiveness. This involves human freedom. It is of course significant for any form of the sacrament of penance. In the early medieval period such a view of human life had to come up against deeply ingrained Celto-Germanic notions of fate and predetermined destiny. This Celto-Germanic matrix left little room for freedom and so for the recognition of sin and, along with that, repentance.

This notion of fate held that culture in its grip. It was a psychological and cultural prison which impeded the penetration of the gospel into that culture and its members. Fate or a predetermined destiny gave enormous power to the past: it seemed to determine human life in such a way that freedom was severely minimised. But the Christian gospel traced out a future promised by God which evoked action and change in human beings.[13] This was the context within which saints such as St Boniface would cut down the sacred oaks which were the meeting point of 'that which determined fate' and the world of human beings.

In the light of this, authors speak of the difficulty the Germanic peoples had in believing that the past could disappear in an act of forgiveness.[14] They could not be so easily unshackled from the power of the past. This led to a sense that one had somehow to pay for one's release from the past. It could not just be received. This was not an idea that people recognised clearly or could identify but it was a part of the mentality within which they lived and which influenced their behaviour preconsciously. This mind or mentality influenced the Christianity of the time, just as the gospel was at work at the same time seeking to transform that mentality. In early medieval terms this left behind a sense that forgiveness had to be paid for. Some scholars suggest that this mentality stretches well up into the later Middle Ages.[15] Indeed, it may be that this is deeply rooted in the human mind generally. It is certainly present in a penitential system like tariff penance which sets a 'price' for every sin.

Charles M. Radding, in a most useful article concerned with the very notion of mentalities, gives the following example to bring out the power of a mentality precisely in the area of our concern – sin and forgiveness:

> In a paper dealing with the historical study of mentalities Jacques Le Goff has cited a story of Gregory the Great (c. 590-600) concerning a monk of his abbey who on his deathbed admitted to having hidden three gold coins in violation of the rule. When informed of this, Gregory ordered that the monk be left to die alone without any consoling word so that the monk would be purged of his sin and his death in anguish would serve as an example to other monks. 'Why' Le Goff asked, 'did not this abbot, who was cultivated and instructed as much as one could be then, go to the bed of the dying sinner to open for him the door of heaven by

confession and contrition? The idea forced itself upon Gregory that one must pay for one's sin by exterior signs: an ignominious death and burial (the body was thrown on the dunghill). Barbarian practice (brought by the Goths or revived from ancient psychic depths?) prevailed over the rule. Mentality conquered doctrine.'[16]

A distorted mentality can often and easily replace gospel without our being explicitly aware of it!

The structure of the penitential system of the tariff is about satisfaction; it is not in the first instance structured according to contrition or confession or forgiveness but, rather, according to satisfaction, the doing of penance. It conceives sin and its repair in much more objective terms than does the later medieval system of penance which, as we will see, concentrates much more on contrition and confession. Early medieval penance is about a wrong thing done and repaired rather than about the subjective intention of the sinner. Underlaying each of these forms of penance is a particular mentality.

The Penitentials present a system of tariffed satisfactions which, in contrast to Germanic law, did emphasise personal responsibility and did begin to change the value systems of the Germanic peoples.[17] However, they remained a system of satisfactions to which contrition, confession and reconciliation were subject, and this in itself conveyed a message at the preconscious level which re-affirmed the 'need-to-pay-a-price' mentality. The very principle of compensation built into the Brehon laws of Ireland which influenced the Penitentials, and which was the mentality enshrined in the *wergeld* principle of Germanic law codes, created an inevitable parallel between the Penitentials and the accepted codes of compensation used by the peoples of the time.

There is another important point to be made about the context of this penitential system and it concerns the practices of commutation and redemption. From our contemporary point of view, these practices seem odd indeed because we feel that an individual cannot pass on their responsibility to anyone else. We do need to note however that our point of view is a long way along the line of development of Western cultures in which the notion of the individual emerges. These penitential practices would not have seemed strange to a person of the early Middle Ages whose sense of solidarity with kin, clan and tribe was as highly developed as is our sense of the individual. In medieval society people were not conceived of in terms of individuals but in terms of their solidarity with each other as a group. As J.C. Russell puts it in describing early medieval Europe:

> ... it was incumbent upon each man and woman of the community to adhere to the fundamental socio-biological principle of group survival embedded in the bonds of familial and communal solidarity ...[18]

This applied to infringements of law and satisfactions which had to be made for them; the whole bonded group was liable for the compensation required of any individual member since he or she was not conceived of outside those relational bonds. Thus redemption of penance done by others who were related to an offending individual made sense to early medieval people in a way which does not make sense to us.

Notes

1. T. M. Charles-Edwards, *Early Christian Ireland* (Cambridge University Press, 2000) 182-271; Hugh Connolly, *The Irish Penitentials* (Dublin: Four Courts Press, 1995) 2-17; Patrick J. Geary, *Before France and Germany* (New York/Oxford: Oxford University Press, 1988) 169-78; Michael S. Driscoll, 'Penance in Transition: Popular Piety and Practice', in Lizette Larson-Miller, ed., *Medieval Liturgy: A book of essays* (New York/ London: Garland Publishing Inc., 1997) 121-63.

2. Geary, *Before France*, 169.

3. John Dallen, *The Reconciling Community* (New York: Pueblo Publishing Company, 1986) 100 -38; Cyrille Vogel, *Il peccatore*

e la penitenza nel medioevo (Turin: Leumann, 1988); Louis-Marie Chauvet, 'Évolutions et révolutions du sacrement de la réconciliation', in Louis-Marie Chauvet and Paul De Clerck, dir., *Le sacrement du pardon entre hier et demain* (Paris: Desclée, 1993) 33-9.

4. Bernard Sesboüé, 'Pardon de Dieu, conversion de l'homme et absolution par l'église', in Louis-Marie Chauvet and Paul De Clerck, dir., *Le sacrement du pardon entre hier et demain* (Paris: Desclée, 1993) 163; Connolly, *The Irish Penitentials*, 18.

5. Connolly, ibid., 30-6.

6. Vogel, *Il peccatore*, 23.

7. ibid., 24.

8. ibid., 24.

9. Paul F. Palmer, *Sacraments and Forgiveness*. Sources of Christian Theology II (Westminster, MD: The Newman Press/ London: Darton, Longman and Todd, 1959) 126.

10. Vogel, *Il peccatore*, 283.

11. John T. McNeill and Helena M. Gamer, ed., *Medieval Handbooks of Penance* (New York: Columbia University Press, 1990) 401.

12. ibid., 402. For another interpretation of the burning of the Penitentials, see Sarah Hamilton, *The Practice of Penance, 900-1050* (Woodbridge, Suffolk: The Royal Historical Society/The Boydell Press, 2001) 6. Hamilton suggests that only the Penitentials that the bishops did not approve of were burnt.

13. James C. Russell, *The Germanization of Early Medieval Christianity* (New York/Oxford: Oxford University Press, 1994) 162-3.

14. Russell, *The Germanization*, 177-8.

15. Mary C. Mansfield, *The Humiliation of Sinners: Public penance in thirteenth century France* (Ithaca/ London, Cornell University Press, 1995) 55-9.

16. Charles M. Radding, 'Evolution of Medieval Mentalities: A cognitive-structural approach', *American Historical Review* 83, 577-97; see 594.

17. Russell, *The Germanization*, 159-61; Peter Brown, *The Rise of Western Christendom* (Cambridge, MA/ Oxford: Blackwells Publishing, 1996) 148-66.

18. Russell, *The Germanization*, 115-29.

Chapter 3

The Middle Ages: Continuity with the Past

In the first two chapters we have examined in some detail the two traditions of penance which laid the groundwork for the future practices of the Church. As we will see, these practices cannot be reduced to the two early traditions but they are dependent on them and develop elements of them.

The medieval forms of penance reflect the medieval world, which was a civilisation arising out of the union of the Germanic peoples who had emigrated into Europe and the established Celtic and Roman population. It was a world becoming Christian over a period of several centuries in a fairly piecemeal fashion. It had a nostalgia for the culture of the old Roman Empire and a desire to imitate Roman ways. It often sought to re-create that past. The Church was the source of the gospel in its midst and the strongest civilising agent at work in the culture; the Church also handed on elements of the old Roman civilisation. This newly forming culture emerged in the aura of ancient Christian Rome even if its perception of it was often what we would call 'romantic'.

In this first chapter on the Middle Ages, the emphasis will be on forms of penance derived from the past, on the persistence of earlier ways into the Middle Ages. As background to understanding penance in this period we need to look at some of the characteristics of the medieval world which influenced its practices of penance. One of these characteristics was its profoundly regional character. There was little emphasis on uniformity, and centralisation was an impossibility given the difficulties of travel and communications.

Peter Brown, in his book, *The Rise of Western Christendom*, describes the earlier centuries of the Middle Ages as a 'period of profound regionalization' and refers to these regions as 'micro-Christendoms'. He is speaking specifically of the seventh century but what he has to say applies, *mutatis mutandis*, beyond that time:

> By the seventh century, the decline of trading networks in the Mediterranean and the hardening of political and confessional boundaries in the Middle East ensured that, despite the enthusiastic movements of a few distinguished travellers, the Christian Churches had become profoundly regionalized. Christianity was a patchwork of adjacent, but separate, 'micro-Christendoms'. No longer bathed, unconsciously, in an 'ecumenical' atmosphere based upon regular inter-regional contacts, each Christian region fell back upon itself. Each needed to feel that it possessed, even if in diminished form, the essence of an entire Christian culture. Often singularly ill-informed about their neighbors, or deeply distrustful of them, the leaders of each 'micro-Christendom' fastened with fierce loyalty on those features that seemed to reflect in microcosm, in their own land, the imagined, all-embracing macrocosm of a world wide Christianity.[1]

Each of these regions tended to see themselves as a microcosm of the whole. This often involved the attempt to recreate Rome in their own place: 'so Wilfrid's Hexham was to be a "Rome" placed within reach of the northern Saxons'.[2] This explains the attempt in many of the great archiepiscopal sees to reproduce the Roman stational system of churches.[3] Thus there was a relationship to Rome as ecclesiastical model, which tuned in with the fascination for Rome which the barbarian peoples had felt ever since their first incursions into the Empire.

The profoundly regional character of the earlier centuries of the Middle Ages can help us understand the existence of varied patterns of liturgical activity throughout the Middle Ages coupled with the importation of Roman liturgical books to provide exemplars for reform. We can see a classical instance of this at the time of the Carolingian reform. The prime movers of that reform – Charlemagne and Alcuin – had a veneration for Roman liturgical books which led them to seek copies of them from Rome and to use them in the Frankish Kingdom. Yet liturgical customs preceding the importation of the Roman books persisted and were used to supplement the Roman books where they were deemed to be deficient according to Northern practice. Liturgical structures and customs received from the past were highly venerated, especially if they came from Rome, the great model, but their use was localised and liturgical authority was embodied in the metropolitan bishop of the local region.[4]

The Middle Ages is a very long period of time – from the sixth century down to the fifteenth/sixteenth centuries. There is scarcely a practice in the life of the Church which remains unchanged over so long a period of time and the Middle Ages was in fact a period in which profound changes occurred in the historical reality of Christianity. With regard to the life of conversion or penance there were many practices at work, many voices speaking on the topic; there were uncertainties in its regard as well as considerable developments, as we shall see. We need to be aware that this was not a static but a very dynamic period in the history of the Church. The practices and developments cannot be neatly ordered because they occurred regionally and in a piecemeal fashion. Because of these features of the Middle Ages it is of interest and importance to us today.

Finally, as mentioned earlier, in relation to the whole history of penance, we need to remember that the listing of the seven sacraments as we have them today began to occur around the middle of this period. General acceptance of that list only occurred in the twelfth century, following the lead of the Parisian theologian, Peter Lombard.[5]

Before Peter Lombard there had been various lists of the rites considered 'sacraments'. Going back further to the first centuries of the Middle Ages and to the Patristic Age, many things were described as sacraments beyond those we would so describe today. Almost any formal, ritual activity of the Church was called a sacrament. The two rites which had been singled out as of greater importance from at least the time of St Augustine were Eucharist and baptism because of both their prominence in the New Testament narratives and their importance in the life of the Church.

Thus what we may call for the sake of clarity the Church's 'institutions of penance' fell into the general area of Church ritual. Only later was penance regarded as a 'sacrament' in the more specific sense of the term to which we are accustomed. This meant that the penitential practices or institutions that we will discuss in this chapter are left in the more diffuse and undifferentiated realm of the Church's ritual activity rather than the more specific, sacramental understanding of the seven sacraments which prevailed from the twelfth century on.

In Lombard's naming of the seven sacraments and in the acceptance of his list by the major theologians who followed him, such as St Thomas Aquinas and St Bonaventure, a new mentality came about which extolled the seven rites called sacraments at the expense of the other ritual actions of the Church; these came to be seen merely as sacramentals, that is, as merely signs, and not causes, of grace.

We must not read this difference between the seven sacraments and other rites of the Church back into the centuries before the general acceptance of such a distinction. People in those earlier times did not see such a great difference between those rites later named as sacraments and the other rites of the Church, except in the cases of baptism and Eucharist. These rites were seen as part of the Church's formal, ritual activity and as being powerful as such. If much of that ritual was more regional than universal, that made little difference to the attitudes of both clergy and laity in their regard.

This caution regarding earlier times is important in regard to penance because several rites used in the penitential life of the Church were part of this overall ritual activity but would not necessarily be assumed into the newer category of the seven sacraments. I will use the term 'penitential institution' of the Church when dealing with these rites.

Penance in the Carolingian reform

Associated with Charlemagne, the first Emperor of the renewed Empire in the West, was the reform of the Church named 'Carolingian', after his dynasty. This occurred in the late eighth and early ninth centuries and one if its concerns was the practices of penance. The aim of the reform of the Church's penitential practice was to return to the ancient canons and so to reinstate the ancient form of canonical penance. This led to the rejection and then the burning of the Penitential Books of Irish tariff penance, as it was considered an illegitimate practice.

As we saw in the previous chapter, in 813, there was a series of local councils – at Chalons-sur-Soane, Tours, Arles, Mainz and Rheims – which, under the stimulus of the Carolingian reform, condemned the Irish practice of penance and sought to promote ancient canonical penance. In each of these councils distinctions were made between public and private sin. It was public sin which must be subject to the ancient canons. In Canon 33 of the Council of Chalons-sur-Soane, it was urged that other sins be confessed either to God or to a priest.[6] This same distinction was made at the Councils of Arles and Rheims.[7]

There is another dispute woven into this larger dispute concerning the confession of non-public sins to a priest.

Such confession to a priest was not part of the practice of the ancient canons and so, apparently, some were opposing it.[8] However the heightening of the priest's role was a principle of the Carolingian reform; so, in this matter, councils defended this innovation, asserting that although these other sins are forgiven by confessing them to God, confession to a priest teaches 'how these same sins may be purged away'.[9] The priest's role was one of teaching and of healing.

An insight into the situation at the time may be given by the following contrast which was mentioned in the previous chapter. On the one hand, Church councils were urging a return to the ancient canonical practice and a council such as the one in Paris in 829 urged the burning of the Penitential Books; on the other hand, as Cyrille Vogel notes: not only did these measures fail to halt the spread of tariff penance but the time of these councils coincided with the period of the greatest production of Penitential Books. The spread of tariff penance in fact continued despite the statements of these councils and their support by the emperor.

What eventually emerged from the Carolingian reform was a double form of penance. We saw this in the distinction between public and private sins made by the Councils of Chalons-sur-Soane, Arles and Rheims. From this emerges an axiom regarding the medieval practice of penance: For grave public sin, public penance; For grave secret sin, secret penance.[10] That is, let public sin be dealt with according to the ancient canons and let secret sin be dealt with according to the tariffs of the Penitentials. Notice that the point of differentiation was not gravity but notoriety. It was specifically the public character of the sin which called for public penance. Such public sin will later be described as sin which disturbs the whole Church.[11] This principle sets up one dimension of the medieval practice of penance.

There are another two characteristics of penance which arose from the Carolingian reform. The first – already mentioned – was that the priest was to be a major figure in all the plans for the reform of the Church: it aimed to reform the Church by reforming the priesthood.[12] Everything became more concentrated in the hands of the priest. So, telling one's sins to God or confessing to a monk or another lay person were customs that would gradually fade away, whereas confessing to a priest would become the only normally accepted form of confessing one's sins.

The second of these other two characteristics to arise was that absolution or reconciliation began to be given immediately after the acknowledgment of one's sins and before the completion of one's imposed penance. This is first formally attested to in the Romano-Germanic Pontifical, about the middle of the tenth century.[13]

Penance in the Middle Ages

It is customary to speak of a threefold institution of penance in the Middle Ages. First, there was *solemn public penance*, which was a continuation of the traditional canonical penance, for public sins; secondly, there was *non-solemn public penance*, which normally involved pilgrimage and was imposed for grave sins which were not so publicly notorious as to require solemn public penance; and, thirdly, there was *private penance*, which was a continuation of tariff penance for sin which was not public. The existence of a triple division of penance in the Middle Ages is commonly accepted today. First appearing in the 1160s, its roots too were in the Middle Ages.

Recent research however warns us that although such a triple division is a suitable way to present the complexity of the penitential institutions of the Middle Ages, we ought also to be aware that it is not to be taken as an exhaustive description of medieval penitential practice. It is a helpful schema though because it shows the continuity with the Carolingian reform and it does indicate the general tendencies and directions of medieval penance.[14]

Solemn public penance

Solemn penance, in various modifications, is quite significant throughout the Middle Ages. The medievals inherited this form of penance from the ancient Church through the Gelasian Sacramentary of the eighth century; its sources, in turn, go back to at least the seventh century. This Sacramentary was known especially in its Frankish forms and came down into the later Middle Ages through the Romano-Germanic Pontifical of the tenth century, along with the regulations of Regino of Prum (d. 915).[15]

This form of penance was to be used only for serious public sin. It was based on Lent: penitents were received on Ash Wednesday, when they were covered with ashes and dressed in sackcloth, and they were reconciled on Holy Thursday by being received back into the celebration of the Eucharist by the bishop. The time between Ash Wednesday and Holy Thursday was the period during which they were to do their prescribed penance. Usually such penances consisted of various measures of the three traditional forms of penance: prayer, fasting and almsgiving.

There is evidence that this penance was not always of one Lenten season's duration but that, in Northern France at least, this could take seven years. Such a penitential process was called the 'carena', and during its long course a gradual reconciliation with the Church occurred. The Frankish books eventually added a new rite for reception back into the Eucharist at the end of the seven years.[16]

This rite of solemn penance was far from being a dead letter. The research of recent scholars reveals the presence of these rituals in the pontificals of at least the major churches of Northern France. Not only are they present in these liturgical books but the evidence is that they were in continuous use. If we take the sequence of pontificals from about 1150 to 1350, we find that the rites were being constantly modified and adapted to differing practical circumstances. The historian, Mary Mansfield, comments:

Evidence from liturgical books is a little more open to challenge, because sometimes scribes with respect for old ways and prayers copied rites, such as royal coronations, not actually practiced in that city. But no taste for the antiquarian can explain why some fifty scribes of Northern French pontificals tinkered with more than forty different versions of public penance from 1150 to 1350, nor why so many in the same period troubled to make marginal additions or changes to the rites already copied. Surely the constant innovation and adjustment in the Lenten rites meant that these were no museum pieces.[17]

These rites did not stultify. Scribes rearranged prayers and rites as if they were not content with them. There was variety in different places and, in any given place, the rites evolved.[18] Not only do we have evidence for this in the rites themselves but we can find descriptions of these rites by authors who witnessed their liturgical use.[19]

These rites were still in use prior to and well after the Fourth Lateran Council and they were being celebrated in that heartland of the medieval world – Northern France, with Paris as its increasingly important point of focus. It is also of interest to note that it was in this same area of Northern France that the impulse for a new form of private penance emerged; this will be the subject of the next chapter.

Public penance was considered more truly sacramental by theologians of the time. Its irrepeatability was evidence of this greater sacramental character, or, as Peter Lombard would say, it could not be repeated *pro reverentia sacramenti* (out of reverence for the sacrament).[20] Theologians of the thirteenth century, such as Albert the Great, simply assumed this greater sacramentality of public penance.

Developments in public penance

Beginning in the eighth century, there were quite significant developments of the public form of penance which broadened the penitential dimension of the Church's life.

As we saw above public penance was based on Lent. It was also a public rite of the Church: the whole assembly of the Church was in principle directly involved in these rites, which were primarily directed to public penitents. The penitents, as we have seen, were regarded as symbolising the Church in need of repentance.

• From public penitents to the whole community

From the association of public penance with Lent and from the presence of the assembled Church at these rites, the people as a whole became more directly involved in them. That is, the wider community of the Church – both laity and clergy – began to participate in the public rites of entry into penance and, later, the rite of reconciliation, in terms of their own sinfulness. Thus on Ash Wednesday, when the public penitents underwent the rite of entry into penance by receiving ashes, the whole assembly began to receive ashes with the penitents. This shift occurred earlier in Northern Europe than in the South where evidence for it cannot be dated earlier than the eleventh century. The people also acknowledged their sins and received a general absolution.[21] This absolution was usually given separately from that given to the public penitents. As time went on, the distinction between the two types of penitents was obscured. This seems to have been the case in some pontificals and sacramentaries of the ninth and tenth centuries.[22]

In some places people made their general confession on Ash Wednesday and were reconciled by an absolution on Holy Thursday separate from that given to the public penitents. In other places the people received absolution straightaway on Ash Wednesday.[23] This kind of rite has a long history. Mary Mansfield states: 'In the North the rite of public penance evolved but survived … the new collective penitential rites for the ordinary faithful supplemented rather than supplanted the old individual public penance'.[24]

From the twelfth century on, there was an interesting development in these rites. Again, according to Mansfield: 'the public now busied themselves with their individual salvation while watching the humiliation of their fellows'.[25] So there was still a link between the penitents and the rest of the assembly but there came about a new concentration on the individual situation of each member of the assembly.

• From Lenten rite to other rites

A further development in these rites occurred in the separation of the rites of penance and reconciliation for all the people from the Lenten rite associated with public penitents. This seems to have occurred in at least three stages.

First, when a bishop, abbot or priest visited a church other than the cathedral church, they used a form of this rite which enabled a greater range of people to take part in penance and reconciliation. In this way a rite of confession and reconciliation for all the people gained autonomy.[26]

Secondly, such rites of general confession and reconciliation were given on great occasions or feasts. Such occasions, as are recorded, were the blessing of a new church or the conclusion of a diocesan synod.[27] On such great occasions the people were encouraged to receive Communion and the rites of general confession and reconciliation were probably a prelude to that Communion.

The third significant development was the appearance of these rites in association with Easter. This third variant appeared especially in priests' manuals so it would seem that they were a matter of parish usage. This could be a specific application of the first stage of the development of these rites described above. Yet again we find this practice particularly in Northern France. Even as far into the Middle Ages as the fifteenth century we find rites of general confession and absolution in use in as many as twenty-one

French dioceses. They could take place on Holy Thursday, another day of Holy Week or even at the Easter Sunday Mass itself. Its use however was still strictly reserved to Lent. It was celebrated in the vernacular.[28] These general confessions took the form of a long list of sins which was read out for the people so that they could recall and recognise their own. A general absolution was then given. This was a reasonably widespread practice involving large numbers of people. Its ultimate origin was solemn public penance.

• Theological Evaluation

How would these rites have been evaluated theologically in their time, bearing in mind that they belong to a quite different period of the Church's life from that which has prevailed from the time of the Reformation and the Council of Trent?

Morinus, a liturgical scholar of the post-Reformation period, said of these rites that they were not *nuda et eximinis ceremonia; sed vera realisque peccatorum remissio,* that is, they are not bare and useless ceremonies but a true and real remission of sins.[29] There are several things we need to take into account in evaluating them. First, they were a part of the instituted life of the Church in its dealing with sin, penance and forgiveness for many centuries. No significant objections were made to them in their own times. Reservations about them and limitations to them were stated in a later period after the practices and the mentality of the Church had changed and individual confession and absolution had become the norm; this was some decades after the Fourth Lateran Council (1215).

Secondly, the spirit of the Church's penitential liturgy, found in the ancient canonical form of penance and in those forms of penance derived from it, was that the Church came before God, interceding for the penitent. That intercession was the specific and powerful intercession of the whole community, which was the body of Christ. This relationship to Christ was the power of its intercession: it was the Church at prayer. This was abundantly clear in the forms of ancient and early medieval penance. The prayer of the Church found expression in the prayer of the penitents, the prayer of the community of the faithful, the prayer of the bishop. The form in which sinners were reconciled was the form of prayer. What would later be called the formula of absolution took the form of prayer for forgiveness and it was a prayer, not a declaration, as would be the case later in the Church's history.[30]

So the expression of reconciliation or absolution in these earlier rites was 'of a piece' with the rest of the rite in its being in the liturgical form of prayer. Just as every part of the rite was a part of the Church's prayer and was expressed as such, so was the culmination of the rite: the expression of the reconciliation of sinners.

Added to this, as outlined at the beginning of this chapter, the Church of the earlier part of the Middle Ages did not think in terms of the seven sacraments and then the other rites as mere sacramentals. Instead, it thought in terms of a whole range of rites which had yet to be categorised as being either sacraments or sacramentals. There was both gain and loss in that subsequent categorisation.

Another significant point (to be dealt with later) is that forgiveness according to Abelard and his contemporaries of the twelfth century – and St Thomas Aquinas would follow this line – was present when contrition was present in the heart of the penitent. Those who were contrite were ipso facto forgiven and that very contrition was a gift of God. Thus any rite in which this redemptive contrition was liturgically expressed and aroused in the hearts of the faithful was effective in the forgiveness of sin.

• Lent

Before moving on to deal with the other branches of medieval penance, we need to note that solemn public penance bequeathed Lent to the Church. Lent in its origins was a baptismal season established by the Fathers of the Church in the fourth century to encourage catechumens to complete their baptismal journey. As Lent passed down into the Middle Ages, it – like the whole Church – moved from having a strong baptismal association to having a strong penitential one. Without any particularly conscious decision, Lent became the season when Christians everywhere joined penitents in their doing of penance by prayer, fasting and almsgiving. Lent became the particular season – though not the only one in the Middle Ages – for the exercise of the virtue of penance or repentance and eventually, in one form or another, for the use of the sacrament of penance.

Non-solemn public penance

The second branch of medieval penance was for those sins which were serious but not of such notoriety as to be considered a sufficient disturbance to the Church or the realm for the Church to call for the use of solemn public penance. The major element in this form of penance was pilgrimage. There may also have been other forms of penance imposed by bishops, priests or other, ecclesiastical bodies. Such other penances as we have evidence for were, for instance, that imposed upon a murderer who had to dig up the corpse of his (or her) victim with his own hands and then bury it again with his own hands. For some offences the perpetrator had to go in procession to a local church and receive his or her punishment there, before the whole population. This punishment had a vague relationship to pilgrimage but did not involve having to leave one's native area.

Pilgrimage

Pilgrimage was a significant part of medieval life and penance. Not all pilgrimages were strictly speaking penitential: some were intercessory, some were done in thanksgiving, some were done for adventure! Pilgrimage was an activity which could be very attractive to people in a society in which most never left their own native place.

The penitential pilgrimage had no roots in the canons of ancient penance but was prominent among the practices of tariff penance. Both pilgrimage and, related to it, exile, were among the serious penances of the Irish system. Pilgrimage had deep roots in the Irish psyche as an act of dedication and conversion. So, along with the ancient canonical penance which became solemn public penance, a strict penance of the tariff system fell into place as an alternative way of dealing with serious sin in the medieval world.

Pilgrimage was imposed for the non-notorious serious sins of the laity and the serious sins of the clergy. Pilgrimage might be imposed for such sins as fornication by a cleric, fornication between monks and nuns, parricides or fratricides, theft from a Church or incest.

Pilgrimage as a penance could be imposed by any parish priest, bishop or other ecclesiastical body. It was ritualised by the presentation of the pilgrim's staff, hat and bag to those being put under penance.[31]

Pilgrimage had the great advantage of getting the offender away from the scene of their serious sin and so of calming the local situation. It involved a form of exile, temporary or permanent. There were two stages in the use of pilgrimage as a penance. The first was its use as a penance for serious sin within the tariff system. The second was its use as non-solemn public penance throughout the Middle Ages. Initially pilgrimage was imposed as a permanent state with no specified destination: penitents were actually put into a state of vagabondage; they were stripped of their links to any particular place and kin group. This introduced pilgrims into a permanent in-between state. They were like Cain, destined to wander the earth after he had killed his brother.

From the ninth century on, there arose more limited forms of pilgrimage in which specific destinations were indicated. A pilgrimage might be *ad Papam* (that is, to Rome), or to the Holy Land, or to Compostella or to numerous shrines of lesser importance, distant or local. Pilgrims were sent off – at times in chains – to make their way to their given destination. As they wandered they had the right to a place at the hearth, and to bread and water at monasteries and shrines along their way.

The reality of pilgrimage in fact, if not in intention, became a permanent scandal of medieval Christianity because it often gathered together some of the most criminal members of both the clergy and the laity. They became a threat to the peace and security of the medieval roads and to the undefended and isolated.

Despite the strictness and the heavy losses involved by those who undertook this form of penance, it was preferable to the penalties of secular law which so often involved mutilation or even capital punishment. Offenders often sought to submit to penance to avoid the drastic effects of being sentenced to such penalties by the law courts.

There were also other significant developments – formal and informal – of the penitential pilgrimage. The Crusades were a formal development of the pilgrimage explicitly presented as its equivalent by Urban II in his calling of the First Crusade at the Council of Clermont in 1095.[32]

Another significant development in the later Middle Ages which is related to pilgrimage, and perhaps also to the penitential processions to local Churches mentioned above, was the flagellant procession. The first recorded instance of such a procession was in 1260. Such processions were never officially sanctioned, much less instituted by Church authorities, but were part of a popular movement which gained considerable momentum as the agricultural and economic reverses of the early thirteenth century set in, followed by the devastations of the Black Death. Participants in such processions sought, by their blood-letting penance, to acknowledge sin and to turn aside the anger of God.

Private Penance

The third branch of medieval penance was private penance. This penance was used for private serious sins or sins of a lesser nature. The origins of this form of penance would seem to be in Irish tariff penance. As time moved on, a private form of penance emerged which had no relationship to the Penitential Books because, as we will see in the next chapter, the element of doing penances or satisfaction tended to diminish in the practice of penance, giving ground to a new mentality based on the confessing of one's sins. Satisfaction, so central to tariff penance, would be considered necessary but secondary in this new type of penitential institution.

Even though tariff penance would seem to be the obvious point of origin for this third form of penance, we cannot ignore the research of scholars indicating the presence in Europe of forms of private penance, of 'confession' of an uncertain nature, *before* the arrival of the Irish monks.[33]

In particular, Cyrille Vogel's research has shown that there was a practice of the confession of sins as a means of freeing the conscience from its burden of sinfulness which was separate from the practices of Irish penance. This form of 'confession', responding to the needs of a troubled conscience, could have been made privately or could have occurred on some relevant public occasion. This practice, which was of a spiritual and therapeutic nature, probably fell into place alongside the Irish practice. It had probably preceded it though we have no accurate idea of the scale of its use. It has in common with the later practice of confession the centrality of the act of confessing one's sins which tariff penance did not have.

It also seems that some Gallic bishops began the practice of giving some form of reconciliation following a confession of sins. This was by word or gesture or both and there is no accompanying mention of the doing of penance or satisfaction. Vogel gives examples of such a practice from as early as the sixth century.

Practices of private penance became more common as the Middle Ages progressed. In the next chapter we will deal specifically with its development into modern penance, appropriately named 'confession'.

The ritual used for private penance in the earlier part of the Middle Ages was a richer and far more complex rite than the one which developed after Lateran IV: it was scaled down and reduced in length so that it could be used more easily. One form of the earlier rite of private penance is given in the Romano-Germanic Pontifical of 950. It had the following pattern. The penitent presented him- or herself to the confessor who went aside to pray and then returned to the penitent to pray over him or her. The confessor made sure that the penitent knew the Lord's Prayer and the Creed and the central doctrines of the faith and questioned him or her on his or her readiness to forgive others. Psalms and prayers were said. The penitent confessed his or her sins, received a penance and was exhorted to renewal of life by the priest. The priest received the prostrate penitent and further prayers followed. Then Mass might follow. This was a rite adapted from the rite of reconciliation for penitents according to the ancient canons with the insertion of the recounting of sins and the giving of penance, a practice derived from tariff penance. There was immediate reconciliation. Vogel estimates that this rite would have taken twenty to thirty minutes, depending on the circumstances, without including the time it would have taken to celebrate Mass if that were to follow.

To summarise this chapter we can say that there was a very considerable mix of practices going on in the life of the Church in the medieval period. Sarah Hamilton in her research, which has been quoted several times throughout this chapter, says that one cannot describe this period as a simple transition from tariff penance to confession; rather, she says: 'no such switch occurred in the period 500-1050: public penance, "secret" penance and forms of mixed penance, of not so formal nor so secret penance continued to be important'.[34]

Notes

1. Peter Brown, *The Rise of Western Christendom* (Cambridge, MA/ Oxford: Blackwell Publishers, 1996) 218. See also Sarah Hamilton, *The Practice of Penance, 900-1050* (Woodbridge, Suffolk: The Boydell Press/ The Royal Historical Society, 2001) 22, and Kathleen G. Cushing, *Reform and the Papacy in the Eleventh Century* (Manchester and New York: Manchester University Press, 2005) 9-12.

2. Brown, *The Rise*, 224.

3. V. Berliere, 'Les stations liturgiques dans les ancien villes episcopals', *Revue liturgique et monastique* 5 (1919/1920) 213-6, 242-8; Theodor Klauser, 'Eine Stationsliste der Metzer Kirche aus dem 8 Jahrhundert: wahrscheinliche ein Werke Chrodegangs', *Sesamelte Arbeiten zur Liturgiegeschichte, Kirchengeschichte und Christliche Archeologie* (Munster, 1974) 22-45; Cyrille Vogel, 'Les Échanges liturgiques entre Rome et les pays francs jusqu'a l'époque de Charlemagne', *Settimane di Studio al Centro Italiano di Studi sull'altomedioevo* VII (Spoleto, 1960) 185-285.

4. Theodor Klauser, *A Short History of the Western Liturgy* (Oxford/ New York/ Toronto/ Melbourne: Oxford University Press, 1979) 72-84; Vogel, Échanges, 265-95.

5. Jozef Finkenzeller, *Die Lehre von den Sacramenten im allgemeinen von der Schrift bis zur Scholastik*. Handbuch der Dogmengeschichte. Band IV, Faszikel 1a (Freiburg/ Basel/ Wien: Herder, 1980) 72-4, 119, 158-66; Bernard Leeming, *Principles of Sacramental Theology* (London: Longmans/ Westminster, MD: The Newman Press, 1962) 566-9.

6. John T. McNeill and Helena M. Gamer, ed., *Medieval Handbooks of Penance* (New York: Colombia University Press, 1990) 401.

7. McNeill and Gamer, *Medieval Handbooks*, 399-400.

8. Vogel, *Il peccatore e la penitenza nel medioevo* (Leumann [Torino]: Editrice Elle Di Ci, 1988) 226.

9. McNeill and Gamer, *Medieval Handbooks*, 401.

10. Vogel, *Il peccatore*, 21.

11. Mary C. Mansfield, *The Humiliation of Sinners: Public penance in thirteenth century France* (Ithaca/ London: Cornell University Press, 1995) 27.

12. Vogel, *Il peccatore*, 20–2; John Dallen, *The Reconciling Community* (New York: Pueblo Publishing Company, 1986) 111-8.

13. Hamilton, *The Practice of Penance*, 122-8; Dallen, *The Reconciling*, 115; Mansfield, *The Humiliation*, 176-7.

14. Vogel, *Il peccatore*, 31; Mansfield, ibid., 24.

15. Vogel, ibid., 22; Mansfield, ibid., 176-7.

16. Mansfield, ibid., 26-9, 170; Hamilton, *The Practice of Penance*, 192.

17. Mansfield, ibid., 96-7.

18. ibid., 161.

19. ibid., 97-8.

20. Peter Lombard, *Sententiae* IV, D14, c4.

21. Thomas Talley, *The Origins of the Liturgical Year* (New York: Pueblo Publishing Company, 1986) 222–5; Mansfield, *The Humiliation*, 189–247; A. Eppacher, 'Die Generalabsolution', *Zeitschrift für Katholische Theologie* 90 (1968) 296-308, 385-421, esp. 297-300; Ladislaus Vencser, 'Berwertung der Generalabsolution im Lichte der Bussgeschichte', *Studia Moralia* 15 (1977) 469-82, esp. 474-6; Hamilton, *The Practice of Penance*, 115-6, 118-21, 126-7.

22. Mansfield, *The Humiliation*, 177.

23. Eppacher, 'Die Generalabsolution', 298–9; Vencser, 'Berwertung', 475; Mansfield, ibid., 177, 188.

24. Mansfield, ibid., 188.

25. ibid., 219.

26. Vencser, 475.

27. Eppacher, 'Die Generalabsolution', 306-7; Vencser, 'Berwertung', 471-2.

28. Nicole Lemaître, 'Pratique et signification de la confession communautaire dans les paroisses au XVIe siècle', in Groupe de la Bussière, *Pratiques de la confession* (Paris: Cerf, 1983) 139-64.

29. Eppacher, 'Die Generalabsolution', 300; Lemaître, ibid., 154-5.

30. François Bussini, 'L'intervention de l'assemblee des fideles au moment de la réconciliation des pénitents d'après les trois "postulationes" d'un archidiacre romain di Ve–Vie siècle', *Revue de Science Religieuse* 41 (1967) 29-38; and idem, 'L'intervention de l'èvêque dans la réconciliation des pénitents d'après les trois postulationes d'un archidiacre romain du Ve-VIe siècle', *Revue de Science Religieuse* 42 (1968) 326-38.

31. Mansfield, *The Humiliation*, 132-8; Cyrille Vogel, 'Le pèlerinage pénitentiel', *Revue de Science Religieuse* 38 (1964) 113-52; Hamilton, *The Practice of Penance*, 174-5.

32. Vogel, 'Le pèlerinage', 145-8.

33. Cyrille Vogel, 'La discipline pénitentielle en Gaule des origines au IXe siècle. Le dossier hagiographique', *Revue de Sciences Religieuses* 30 (1956) 1-26, 157-86. Hamilton, *The Practice of Penance*, 4, 13-4.

34. Hamilton, ibid., 209.

Chapter 4

The Middle Ages:
A New Form of Penance: Confession

The long period which we call 'the Middle Ages' is a quite complex and varied stretch of time; it is a period of considerable development and we remain in its debt.

The Church's ritual practices of penance in this period are like a large tree of many branches, some of which we have already examined in the previous chapter. In this chapter we want to look more closely at just one of those branches, one which stretches right down into our own century. This new form of penance, commonly known as 'confession', can rightly be seen as a third tradition in the history of the Church's institutions of penance. The penitential practice of confession was to become one of the identifying marks of modern Catholicism.

During the twelfth century there began a new phase in the history of the sacrament of penance. For some time the Penitential Books of tariff penance had been found to be unsatisfactory because each diverse group of Penitentials gave different penances or tariffs for the same sins; this caused confusion and uncertainty and, more importantly, in view of new and profound influences at work in the culture of the twelfth century, dissatisfaction with the old system arose.

It was during the second half of the twelfth century that the Penitentials fell into disuse as confessors began to adapt penances to the individual penitent's situation.[1] During this same century, theologians were presenting lists of the sacraments, understood in the more precise sense of the term, which would become standard down to our day; penance was listed among these seven.

We can parallel this new attitude towards sacraments to a new attitude towards miracles which arose at the same time. Previously, miracles had not been interpreted as exceptions to the laws of nature but simply as more noticeable instances of the same divine creative activity that was at work in creation all the time. In the twelfth century, with its more empirical temper and the increasing influence of Aristotelian thought, miracles came to be understood as exceptions to the fixed laws of God's creation. In parallel, the seven rites that we call sacraments had previously been understood as among the many rites of the Church through, and in, which God worked, but, in this period, they came to be understood as the seven rites in which God definitely and effectively worked. God's activity was seen as channelled through these seven specific rites.

We can say that by 1180, penance was universally accepted as one of the seven sacraments.[2] Increasingly, as time went on, the sacrament of penance came to mean private penance, that is, private confession and absolution. However, this does not seem to have been the case for quite some time, since, as we have seen, both Peter Lombard and Albert the Great regarded solemn penance as more truly sacramental because of its irrepeatability.[3] It is not at all clear which form (or forms) of the sacrament was intended in the first listings of penance among the seven sacraments.[4]

A new mentality – a new form of penance

The new form of the sacrament of penance arose along with, and as a result of, a new mentality and culture which arose in Europe from the end of the eleventh, and into the twelfth and thirteen, centuries.

One of the threads of this new, rising culture has been identified by historians as the greater importance given to the Individual.[5] An increased sense of individuality and of self-awareness emerged at this time out of an earlier social and psychological situation in which group solidarity was the stronger mood. The new form of penance is an example that historians give of this new culture. For us the process is the reverse: we want to look at this greater emergence of the individual as a help to understanding the rise of a new form of penance.

Authors see the following as signs of the rising sense of the individual at that time. In art, there was a movement from icon to portrait; in the latter, the specific features of individuals were more important than they were in the former. In the presentation of the Person of Christ, his human characteristics were more and more highlighted, so in reading the scriptural narratives commentators were more prone to note how Jesus felt or reacted. Authors see the same emergence of the individual manifested in love poetry and in the greater psychological introspection that is evident in other literature of the time.[6] This same approach and mentality was at work in the writing of lives of the saints. In earlier 'lives' of the saints, what mattered was that the pattern of life of this particular saint fitted into the formula of expectations required for someone to be a saint; in the new 'lives', the interest of authors and readers tended to concentrate upon the specific characteristics of a particular saint's personality and life.[7] The rise of the new form of penance showed the same mentality at work that we see in the above instances.

The thinker who gave expression to the new theology of penance within this new mentality was Peter Abelard (1079-1142). In regard to sin and penance – as in many other areas – his influence has been decisive for subsequent theology. Marie-Dominique Chenu comments that it was Abelard who showed the importance of subjective factors in human behaviour.[8] Abelard asserted the primacy of intention in doing good and in committing sin: it was not just what one did but one's intention in doing it. As a consequence, it was contrition or inner sorrow which was the most important factor in 'achieving' forgiveness; such contrition was the sign of God's forgiveness already at work in human beings. This view so influenced the practice of penance that it would bring about a new era in its history.

The primacy of intention was a revolutionary principle with regard to the Church's institutions of penance and the form in which they would develop because, in both the canonical and tariff systems of penance, the predominant element was the doing of penance or satisfaction in terms of prayer, fasting and almsgiving. They were the acts by which conversion was seen to be brought about, spiritual damage repaired and things set at rights. The emphasis was on objective actions of prayer, fasting, almsgiving and self-denial.

Once Abelard's principle took hold, the tariff system had to fade away because 'penances' in his thinking had to be tailor-made for the penitent and not determined by an arbitrary scale of tariffs which took little account of intention. There was a lessening in the importance of the penance to be done and an emphasis on the contrition evident in the penitent because contrition was the sign that the penitent was already forgiven. The role of the confessor was to ascertain the genuineness of this contrition rather than to calculate the penance or tariff due. The contemporaries of Abelard shared his mentality. Even Abelard's fiercest opponents on other matters, such as St Bernard of Clairvaux, agreed with him on the primacy of intention and contrition.

Chenu, quoted above, goes on to make the following remarks about Abelard's emphasis on the subjective in penance:

> ... at the same time as this there was an awakening of conscience in the Christian people who were being trained slowly and steadily through a general rise in the level

of culture and refining of their hitherto gross personal manners, to engage in personal prayer, examine their conduct and to practice moral criticism.[9]

The historian, Aaron Gurevich, stresses the role of Abelard in providing intellectual grounding to the new tendency towards the interiorisation of the faith and the emphasis on individual responsibility, as opposed to the earlier Christian culture which conceived sin, rather, as an objective evil outside the person themselves which, so to speak, invaded them. Sin so conceived needed to be dealt with ritually because people saw themselves as subject to a power from outside themselves. This, Gurevich suggests, was symbolised in the *ordeal*, but was also expressed in the less dramatic form of having to do a penance entirely determined according to a tariff set up irrespective of the individual. For Abelard, confession and repentance were not significant in that more ritual sense but as the expression of 'sincere emotional distress' resulting from the awareness that a sin had been committed. We can see in this an example of the new cultural and religious awareness of the individual.[10]

Another point of significance is that medieval psychology had a strong emotional tone. The medievals were not 'the restrained gentlemen' of later times; rather, their emotions were transparent. Tearful repentance and prayer for the gift of tears were a part of the religious sensibility of the time. The sinner's knowledge of their sin brought about by self-analysis led to compunction, to distress and to contrition.[11]

Intention

From this new mentality, with its greater awareness of the individual, there arose a new sense of sin and a correspondingly different use of rituals of penance. In this mentality, sin was interpreted as resulting from the intention of the person to sin and so the person had to be brought to penance and forgiven. Contrition therefore became the crucial element of penance because the person who has sinned has to come to grips with that sin as theirs, as something they had intended.

In the new system the sinner needed to recognise themselves as sinner and feel the compunction and contrition arising from that recognition, and then confess the sin involved. Moreover, contrition was not seen simply as part of a human process but as the evidence of divine forgiveness; it was the God-given element in the process which gave meaning to the whole. The 'tears of repentance' were the sign that the penitent was already reconciled.

This new mentality did not contradict those underlying the earlier forms of penance. It had elements in common with them as well as elements that were different. It was another Christian mentality appropriate to the particular shape of the human culture of its day.

Confession

This system of penance is accurately called 'confession' because it was in the act of confessing one's sins that its specific character found expression. This form of penance was a 'psychological dramatisation of the sinner's state by means of the act of confession'.[12] And it was the shame of this confession which was seen as that which had to be endured and so was the equivalent of doing penance. The actual penances to be done became more and more insignificant as time went on because it was the embarrassment of confessing which was the act or doing of penance. This also makes sense of the increasingly frequent giving of absolution before the doing of the penance:

> … the humiliation and the shame involved in this sacrament are so great that the Catholic Church sees in that the principal expiation of the fault, and as often as possible gives absolution immediately after the confession.[13]
> (author's translation)

This new mentality and this new teaching about penance were on the increase throughout the twelfth century. It was increasingly accepted among theologians even if, like Abelard, they did not yet speak of this new form of penance as a sacrament.[14]

From the fact that, on this view, it was contrition which was at the heart of the process of penance, the question arose as to the point of the priest's absolution. The confessor's role was seen at first as being that of ascertaining that contrition was in fact present in the person and the absolution was seen as the confessor's formal recognition of the presence of that contrition.

The priest's role in penance would prove to be a constant question for the theologians of the latter half of the twelfth and the thirteenth centuries.[15] To explain it they would often use scriptural images such as the lepers being cured by Christ but being told to go and show themselves to the priest or that of Lazarus being raised to life by Christ but having to be released from his shroud by Christ's disciples. So a *quoddam ecclesiale* (an ecclesial dimension), as St Thomas would say, was associated with the priest's absolution. This fitted in, *mutatis mutandis*, with the structure of ancient canonical penance. It drew in an element which made ecclesial a practice whose origins were specifically monastic and spiritual.[16]

This new development occurred among the elite of the society of the time. The self-analysis required in confession was demanding and quite impossible for the majority of people. Gurevich comments:

> Scholars focus particular attention on the fact that, at the beginning of the thirteenth century, the confessor acquired new significance: it was laid down in a decision taken by the Fourth Lateran Council (1215) that every Christian should make a confession to a priest once a year. Regular individual and secret confession presupposed self-analysis on the part of the believer: one was required to consider one's behaviour

to decide what was sinful and what was righteous about it. Actual practice sometimes had little to do with analysis of the consciousness of the believer and easily degenerated into profanation of the sacrament of confession, because the majority of believers did not prove able or inclined to carry out self-analysis of this sort, and many confessors were unable to help them, thus reducing the activity to no more than a superficial ritual. Nevertheless, the principle had been established and signified an important stage in the evolution of the Christian's religious awareness.[17]

Confession developed among the elite, both clerical and lay, who were participating in the cultural and religious renewal of the time but it progressed very slowly indeed among the greater number of Christians. The very persistence of other instituted means of dealing with sin and forgiveness, which we saw in the previous chapter, testifies to hesitancy in taking on the new form of penance.

The practice of confessing daily faults as well as serious sin seems to have grown up little by little in the twelfth and thirteenth centuries. The background of this practice would seem to have been in the practices of the monasteries and those of the new mendicant orders. Lay spirituality at the time was normally derived from that of the religious orders and many of the lay elite would have belonged to third orders attached to them.

The practice of confessing as a preparation for receiving Communion increased but confession was also practised quite independently of receiving Communion, as a spiritual exercise with its own spiritual rewards. St Louis IX felt the need to confess whenever he felt that he had sinned.[18] Such a very frequent use of the sacrament took on among some of the devout.

An important point that Gurevich makes in the above quotation is that the parish clergy were soon to be required to be confessors on a regular basis, but they were not able to fulfil this role. Given their formation and state of life, they were incapable of dealing with consciences in the terms that this form of penance required. The problem of forming confessors became particularly acute after the imposition of annual confession and absolution on every Catholic by the Fourth Lateran Council (1215). This confession was to be made to their own parish priest but the inability of priests to be confessors tended to defeat the purpose of the obligation. Eventually, this problem was alleviated to some extent by allowing people to confess to friars. This was allowed by a papal decree of 1281.

An initiative to help the local clergy in their new role as confessors was the production of a new type of book, called the *Summa Confessorum*, the 'Summa for Confessors'. These books were quite different from the old Penitentials. Their aim was to give the confessor guidance in helping the penitent to discover his or her sins and to confess them accurately and then to help the confessor to give advice and choose a suitable penance for the penitent.[19]

A confession mentality

Confession, being the act in which the penitent expressed their contrition and the act in which one experienced the penance of embarrassment, eventually came to be seen as so important that, for many, it was important to confess, even if there was no priest available to hear their confession and give them absolution. Given the historical background of the variety in the forms of penance, and given the facts that: tariff penance, at least in its earlier centuries, could involve a monk who was not a priest; daily sins could be confessed to people other than priests; a less precise mentality prevailed regarding which rituals were sacraments and which were not; and the prevailing uncertainty about the purpose of the priest's absolution, it was not so strange that people in the latter part of the medieval period sought to confess to a lay person in a case of necessity when a priest was not available. The desire to confess would eventually become so prominent in the culture and mentality of the time that the act of confessing came to matter most.

There was also a positive theological appreciation of confession to a lay person. St Thomas Aquinas' thought on this is quite clear in the treatment of penance which we find in the Supplement at the end of his *Summa Theologiae*. The Supplement completes that part of the *Summa* which Thomas had never finished: it was written by his secretary on the basis of earlier works. The first passage of importance reads as follows:

> I answer that, just as Baptism is a necessary sacrament, so is Penance. And Baptism, though being a necessary sacrament has a twofold minister: one whose duty it is to baptise, in virtue of his office, viz. the priest, and another, to whom the conferring of baptism is committed, in a case of necessity. In like manner the minister of Penance to whom, in virtue of his office, confession should be made, is a priest: but in a case of necessity even a layman may take the place of a priest, and hear a person's confession.[20]

The text goes on to say, in reply to an objection, that it is never lawful to confess to another than a priest, but that:

> … when there is a reason for urgency, the penitent should fulfil his own part, by being contrite and confessing to whom he can; and although this person cannot perfect the sacrament, so as to fulfil the part of the priest by giving absolution, yet this defect is supplied by the High Priest. Nevertheless, confession made to a layman, through lack of a priest is quasi-sacramental, although it is not a perfect sacrament, on account of the absence of the part which belongs to the priest.[21]

We find further extension of this desire to confess mentioned by Vogel in his history of penance. When another person was not available to hear one's confession, confession was made to something precious such as one's horse or sword. We can again see in this practice the sheer importance of confessing.[22] Vogel notes that alongside this practice, there was a tendency to receive Viaticum by means of some earthly element other than the eucharistic bread when it was impossible to receive the Eucharist. Vogel mentions such things as a flower or some earth as substitutes.[23]

Confession of venial sin

Another point that is clear in medieval religious practice and in medieval theology is that venial sin is forgiven in many ways apart from the use of confession. St Thomas Aquinas deals with this as follows:

> I answer that, by venial sin man [*sic*] is separated neither from God nor from the sacraments of the Church: wherefore he does not need to receive any further grace for the forgiveness of such a sin, nor does he need to be reconciled with the Church. Consequently, a man does not need to confess his venial sins to a priest. And since confession made to a layman is a sacramental, although it is not a perfect sacrament, and since it proceeds from charity, it has a natural aptitude to remit sins, just as the beating of one's breast, or the sprinkling of holy water. This suffices for a reply to the first objection, because there is no need to receive a sacrament for the forgiveness of venial sins; and a sacramental such as holy water or the like suffices for this purpose.[24]

Here St Thomas is dealing with the question of the forgiveness of venial sins along with that of confession to lay people, as we can see from the text. It is clearly his opinion that venial sin can be forgiven in a multitude of ways. The Council of Trent will put forward the same point.[25] This will be important for our later consideration of the issues which face us in our contemporary use of the sacrament of penance.

Confession – absolution

As we saw above, the emphasis on contrition that was so much at the core of this new form of penance opened up for discussion the purpose of the priest's absolution. Since all the theologians of the latter part of the medieval period essentially agreed with Abelard that true contrition in the penitent was the gift of God's forgiveness already present in them, how was one to explain the value of the priest's absolution?

There were several responses given to this question. Some theologians said that the priest's absolution declared that the contrition in the penitent was authentic and that therefore they were forgiven. Others held that absolution does not forgive sin but takes away any temporal punishment due to sin, that is, it deals with remaining effects of the sin in the person. Others again taught that the priest's absolution transforms the conditional forgiveness of sin in the penitent's heart to an absolute forgiveness.[26]

St Thomas's solution to this problem is based on his general theory of the sacraments, according to which each sacrament is made up of matter and form. So in the Eucharist, the bread and wine are the matter of the sacrament which become the sacrament by being in-formed by the words of Christ spoken by the minister. Likewise, the bridegroom and bride are the ministers of marriage to each other: the words of consent of the bride are the form of marriage for the groom whose words of consent are the matter of the marriage for him; conversely, the groom's words of consent to the bride are the form of marriage for her and her words of consent to him are the matter of marriage for her. In this interplay of matter and form, the sacrament of marriage is constituted.

Similarly for the sacrament of penance, the acts of the penitent – contrition, confession and satisfaction – are the matter of the sacrament, and the words of absolution by the priest are the form of the sacrament. Those words inform the matter to make the sacrament. In Thomas's understanding, it is very clear that the priest's absolution does not by itself constitute the sacrament, as would be the opinion of some later theologians, but that the acts of the penitent and the words of absolution by the priest together constitute the sacrament. The acts of the penitent and the act of the priest interact to form the sacrament. This takes seriously both sides of the interchange; both are essential to the sacrament.

In the time of St Thomas there was a transition occurring from the supplicatory form of absolution (that is, absolution in the form of a prayer) to the declarative form of absolution (such as 'I absolve you from your sins in the name of …'). The supplicatory or prayer form of absolution was derived from those used in ancient canonical penance in which reconciliation (or absolution) was expressed in the form of a prayer by the bishop. Early medieval forms of private penance took over several liturgical elements of ancient canonical penance.

Thomas acknowledges that the declarative form of absolution was barely thirty years old at the time of his writing;[27] nonetheless, he saw the new declarative form as important to his understanding of the sacrament. He sees it as making clear the sacramentality of private penance by reference to the power of the keys. This link between penance and the power of the keys had received relatively little emphasis earlier in the course of the tradition; however, for Thomas, it is the power of the keys which is expressed in the priest's words of absolution. This link is the basis of his theology of absolution. Thomas sees absolution as adding 'an ecclesial dimension' to penance; he refers to a *quoddam ecclesiale*.[28]

If we put this in the context of Thomas's systematisation of the seven sacraments, he is insisting here on an element necessary for the full sacramentality of penance and he does so against a background in which public penance was seen as having a sacramentality superior to that of private penance.[29] This superiority of public penance was grounded in its pedigree as a descendant of ancient canonical penance whose structure showed a full ecclesial dimension. Private penance, however, as we saw above, was a descendant of a monastic and spiritual practice which did not bear all the signs of the ecclesial character required in Thomas's theology. Emphasising the importance of the priest as representing the whole Church gave it the character necessary for its recognition as one of the seven sacraments.

The process of conversion which Thomas sees taking place in the sacrament of penance involves the penitent's union with Christ and the Church; it is an ecclesial, sacramental matter and not a purely individual or purely moral matter. There is a direction to the process going on in the penitent in the very gift of contrition expressed in confession. It is a direction which is informed all the way along by the word of Christ which finds its completion in the words of absolution spoken by the priest. This process of conversion occurs in the penitent only because it is aroused in him or her by the word of Christ. This is a process worked out, carried forward and completed by the informing word of Christ. The words of absolution perfect this process.[30]

The Fourth Lateran Council (1215)

Innocent III called the Fourth Lateran Council in 1215 and its twenty-first canon added a new dimension to the history of penance. It stated that:

> Everyone of the faithful of both sexes after reaching the age of discretion should at least once a year faithfully confess alone all his sins to his own priest, and should attempt to fulfil the penance imposed with all his strength, receiving the sacrament of the Eucharist reverently at least at Easter, unless perhaps by the advice of his own priest for some reasonable cause, he should abstain from receiving it for a time. Otherwise let him be kept from entering the church during his lifetime and on his death let him be denied Christian burial.[31]

This decree canonised the new form of penance which had developed over the preceding century and a half. The decree did not of course appear out of nowhere. It was prepared for by the elite of Christians of the twelfth and thirteenth centuries who were finding the new practice of penance a source of Christian conversion and renewal. The annual usage of individual confession had been promoted by significant bishops who had introduced it into their dioceses during the years preceding the council.[32]

That this practice began to be proposed universally at this time was the result of a reforming impetus begun at the very end of the twelfth century, centred on the University of Paris. The impetus was both expressed and augmented by the above decree of the council enjoining annual confession on all adult Christians.[33] Lateran IV became an official turning point in the history of penance even though its effects would be slow and piecemeal in coming. It was supported by efforts at education especially for confessors, in the *Summae Confessorum*, and by preachers, in their contact with the people.[34] It did issue in a quite radical change in the place of the sacrament of penance in the lives of individual Christians and in that of parish communities.

The decree of Lateran IV introduced in principle the universal practice of annual confession. It did not specify whether that was for all sins or only for serious sins. The confession was to be made to one's own parish priest. This involved quite some difficulty because most people in Europe at the time lived in small village parishes where everyone was known to everyone else. The confession was to occur alone, that is, without others present. Mansfield makes an interesting suggestion for interpreting the word 'alone' in the decree: she sees it over against the custom of a priest celebrating 'private' penance with a small group of people.[35] In Lateran IV's decree there is some emphasis on doing the imposed penance: '… and should attempt to fulfil the penance imposed with all his strength'. The practice is conceived of as oriented to the reception of Communion at Easter, thus affirming the link between confession and Communion.

There is public punishment attached to the non-fulfilment of the annual duty to confess one's sins: '… let him be kept from entering the church during his lifetime and at his death let him be denied Christian burial.' The denial of entry to the Church was a form of exclusion from the community of the Church to which all at that time belonged, just as the refusal of Christian burial was the refusal of entry into the community of those who had died. This placed a fearsome and powerful sanction upon the non-fulfilment of this duty. It also carried some reminiscences of the canonical penance of exclusion.

Lateran IV's obligation set the scene for the next period in the history of penance. As we conclude this chapter with it, so with it we will begin the next.

Notes

1. Pierre-Marie Gy, 'Les bases de la pénitence moderne', *Maison Dieu* 117 (1974) 64-5.

2. Jozef Finkenzeller, *Die Lehre von den Sakramenten im allgemeinen von der Schrift bis zur Scholastik*. Handbuch der Dogmengeschichte. Band IV. Faszikel 1a (Freiburg/ Basel/ Wien: Herder, 1980) 119-22, 158-66; Bernard Leeming, *Principles of Sacramental Theology* (London: Longmans/ Westminster, MD: The Newman Press, 1960) 566-9.

3. Mary C. Mansfield, *The Humiliation of Sinners: Public penance in thirteenth century France* (Ithaca/ London: Cornell University Press, 1995) 32-3. See Peter Lombard, *Sententiae* IV, D 14, c.4; Albert the Great, *Commentarii in IV Sententiarum* IV, D 4, a. 27c.

4. N. M. Häring, 'The Interaction between Canon Law and Sacramental Theology in the Twelfth Century', in Stephen Kuttner, ed., *Proceedings of the Fourth International Congress of Medieval Canon Law (1972)* (Citta del Vaticano, 1976) 489ff.

5. Aaron Gurevich, *The Origins of European Individualism* (Oxford, UK/ Cambridge, USA: Blackwell, 1995); Colin Morris, *The Discovery of the Individual, 1050-1200* (London, 1972); Caroline

Walker Bynum, 'Did the Twelfth Century Discover the Individual?', in idem, *Jesus as Mother: Studies in the spirituality of the High Middle Ages* (Berkeley/ Los Angeles/ London: University of California Press, 1982), 82-108; Marie-Dominique Chenu, *L'éveil de la conscience dans la civilisation médiévale* (Montreal: Institute d'Études médiévales/ Paris: Librairie J. Vrin, 1969).

6. Gurevich, *The Origins*, 5-6.

7. Gurevich, ibid., 12; Jacques Le Goff, *Medieval Civilisation* (Oxford: Basil Blackwell, 1988) 327-9, 329-30.

8. Marie-Dominique Chenu, *Nature, Man and Society in the Twelfth Century* (Chicago/ London: The University of Chicago Press, 1968) 284-5; R. E. Weingart, 'Peter Abailard's Contribution to Medieval Sacramentology', *Recherches de theologie ancienne et medievale (Mt Cesar)* 34 (1967) 159-78.

9. Chenu, *Nature*, 285.

10. Gurevich, *The Origins*, 127-8; Jean Charles Payen, 'La pénitence dans le contexte culturel des XIIe et XIIIe siècles', *Revue des Sciences Philosophiques et Theologiques* 61 (1977) 399-428, see 405-6; Gy, 'Les bases', 66.

11. Payen, *La pénitence dans*, 402-3; Jacques Le Goff, 'Saint Louis et la practice sacramentelle', *Maison Dieu* 197 (1994) 99-124.

12. Jean Delumeau, *La confessione e il perdono* (Cinisello Balsamo [Milano]: Edizioni Paoline, 1992) 16.

13. Delumeau, ibid., 23.

14. Weingart, 'Peter Abailard's contribution', 175-6; Jacques Le Goff, *Your Money or Your Life* (New York: Zone Books, 1988) 11-3.

15. Payen, *La pénitence dans*, passim; Weingart, 'Peter Abailard's contribution', 175-6.

16. Payen, ibid., 422; Eric Luijten, *Sacramental Forgiveness as a Gift of God* (Leuven: Peeters, 2003) 153, 184-9, 210-5; Bernard Sesboüé, 'Pardon de Dieu, conversion de l'homme et absolution par l'église', in Louis-Marie Chauvet and Paul De Clerk, ed., *Le sacrement du pardon entre hier et demain* (Paris: Desclée, 1993) 165-71.

17. Gurevich, *The Origins*, 111-2.

18. Gy, 'Les bases', 73-4.

19. Alexander Murray, 'Confession as an Historical Source in the Thirteenth Century', in R. H. C. Davis and J. H. Wallace-Hadrill,

The Writing of History in the Middle Ages (Oxford) 275-322; Thomas N. Tentler, 'The Summa for Confessors as an Instrument for Social Control', in C. Trinkhaus and C. Oberman, *The Pursuit of Holiness in Late Medieval and Renaissance Religion*, Studies in Medieval and Renaissance Thought, X (Leiden, 1974) 103-37.

20. *S.T.* Supp. Q 8, art 2, Resp.

21. *S.T.* Supp. Q 8, art 2, Ad 1.

22. Cyrille Vogel, *Il peccatore e la penitenza nel medioevo* (Leumann [Torino]: Editrice Elle Di Ci, 1970) 25.

23. Vogel, ibid., 25-6.

24. *S.T.* Supp. Q 8, art 3, Resp, Ad 1.

25. 'Decree on the Sacrament of Penance', Council of Trent, 1551, in Karl Rahner, ed., *The Teaching of the Catholic Church* (New York: Alba House, 1967) n. 564.

26. John Dallen, *The Reconciling Community* (New York: Pueblo Publishing Company, 1986) 140-50; Payen, *La pénitence dans*, passim.

27. *S.T.* Supp Q 84, art 3; 'Absolution' (Formule de l') in *Catholicisme* Vol. 1, cols 59-60.

28. Luijten, *Sacramental Forgiveness*, 210-7.

29. Mansfield, *The Humiliation*, 32-3.

30. Luijten, ibid.

31. DS. Denzinger-Schonmetzer, *Enchiridion Symbolorum, Definitionum et Declarationum de rebus fidei et morum*. Editio XXXIII (Freiburg: Herder, 1965) n. 812.

32. Nicole Bérriou, 'Autour de Latran IV (1215): La naissance de la confession moderne et sa diffusion', Groupe de la Bussière, ed., *Pratiques de la confession* (Paris: Cerf, 1983) 73-94; Mansfield, *The Humiliation*, 67ff.

33. Bérriou, *Autour de Latran IV*, 74-5.

34. Bérriou, ibid., 80ff.

35. Mansfield, *The Humiliation*, 66-7.

Chapter 5

Penance in the Late Middle Ages and the Modern Age

From Lateran IV to the Council of Trent

The Fourth Lateran Council, as we saw in the previous chapter, took up the new form of penance which had developed over the previous one hundred years and imposed it as an annual obligation on every Catholic. Although this practice took quite some time to come into universal effect, Lateran IV took up the recently developed third thread of the tradition of penance and gave it new force by means of its decree. It brought the practice into the life of the Church in a way that had never happened before and so created a new era in the sacrament's history.

In describing this new era, we need to consider, on the one hand, the elite of the Church and, on the other, ordinary Catholics, particularly those living in the villages of Europe who were largely untouched by the renewal of the eleventh and twelfth centuries. For the elite, penance became a central act of their devotional life. They tended to confess all their sins, go to confession frequently and see their recourse to a confessor as a core element in their spiritual life. Going to confession for them was not so much preparation for going to Communion but a spiritual activity in its own right. The historical and liturgical scholar, Pierre-Marie Gy, says such people thought: 'the more one is a Christian, the more one confesses'.[1] This new spirituality was part of a strong devotional movement within the particular religious, cultural and theological setting of the time.

On the other hand, the imposition of this form of penance on every Catholic as an annual practice brought it (one might even say, dragged it) into the life of every Catholic. Thus the practice was expected of people who were not part of the devotional movement behind it. It was expected of the whole Catholic people, among whom it did not find easy acceptance, especially since they had to make this confession to their own parish priest to whom, in most cases, they would be very well known. This practice so desired by the devout took on an entirely different hue once it was imposed on everyone. It was their devotional spirit which made this practice significant to the elite, but that devotion was not present to inspire the practice among the ordinary people.

The reformers and the elite were convinced of the importance and value of contrition, the core of the new practice of penance. The spiritual experience of compunction was a real experience for them. The reformers, in seeking this experience for the whole Church, saw themselves as urging on the Church a great instrument of renewal and conversion. For them Lateran IV's decree was a great victory and a moment for the renewal of the whole Church.

The ordinary Catholic was not capable of the self-analysis required for this practice and, on top of that, their clergy were generally unable to fulfil the demands of their role in this new form of penance. The very imposition of this practice tended to defeat the purpose behind the desired renewal.[2]

Undoubtedly, given the proper conditions, this new practice gave some people beyond the elite an experience of God's forgiveness and of conversion and renewal. But it would seem, from the testimonies available to us, that it was a burden and a problem for the majority. Jean Delumeau, a Catholic historian who has made a significant contribution to the study of the history of penance, offers two useful comments which help us to grasp the effect of this imposition on the whole Church. The first is his suggestion that:

... private and obligatory confession had in the preoccupation of the time (from the thirteenth century on) a place comparable to that occupied today in the media and public opinion by contraception, abortion, the various types of artificial insemination and euthanasia.[3] (author's translation)

And, secondly, Delumeau notes the awareness of this difficulty as shown even by a document of such standing as the Catechism of the Council of Trent: 'for most of the people there are no other days they pass with greater nervousness than those set aside by the Church for confession'.[4] (author's translation)

The whole of Delumeau's previously quoted book gives us a sense of the discomfiture which accompanied this obligatory use of the sacrament in the centuries between Lateran IV and Trent and in the centuries following the Council of Trent. There was a combination of conformity and opposition in the majority of the population. It produced a use of the sacrament which was minimalist and grudging. The Catholic Reformers following the Council of Trent recognised that, although people had been fulfilling their obligation to go to confession annually, it was not very frequently a satisfactory and fruitful use of the sacrament.[5]

The obligation of annual confession raised theological difficulties in its very practice. The first concerned contrition. Although contrition was at the heart of this practice, many people were coming to the sacrament not because of a spontaneous sense of contrition but because of the obligation and the drastic consequences of failing to comply with the obligation: exclusion from the Church while alive and the refusal of Christian burial at death. As a consequence, confessors found difficulty in discerning whether penitents were contrite or not. From this derived another problem: what degree of contrition was necessary for a true confession? Is it enough that the penitent has an imperfect contrition (called 'attrition')? Imperfect contrition would arise from fear of hell, or fear of the consequences of not fulfilling the annual obligation, rather than an authentic compunction. This became a question of considerable theological debate.[6] It was eventually agreed that imperfect contrition was sufficient. However, penance based on imperfect contrition rather changes the character of this form of penance as it was originally conceived on the basis of felt contrition expressed in confession.

There was also the phenomenon which Delumeau calls 'spiritual obstetrics'. How do confessors manage to get the penitent to 'give birth' to their sins, that is, to put them into words in confession? This proved to be a labour for both confessor and penitent.[7]

In the course of these centuries, and partially as a result of the difficulties mentioned above, a shift occurred in the theology of, and mentality behind, the sacrament of penance. It was a shift from an understanding of penance based on contrition which had predominated since Abelard, to an understanding of the sacrament based on absolution as an exercise of the power of the keys. The difficulties experienced by both penitents and confessors were central to this shift. The understanding of the sacrament based on the priest's absolution made the power of the sacrament clearer and more secure and less dependent upon the clarity of the penitent's contrition. In this we see that the theological view of the sacrament developed in the theology of St Thomas Aquinas was also in accord with a pastoral need.

Given the above difficulties, it is no surprise that there is evidence of forms of general confession and absolution persisting into the sixteenth century. It was noted above that these were used in Holy Week or on Easter Sunday itself in order to facilitate the reception of the Easter Communion.[8]

Despite these difficulties and the rather grudging spirit in which penance was so often celebrated, the practice of individual confession of sins and reception of absolution gradually became more widespread in the period following Lateran IV. Efforts following the Council of Trent were more effective in propagating the practice and it became an important element in the Post-Tridentine renewal of Catholic life.[9]

The practice of the annual confession of sins culminating in the reception of Communion at Easter had a strong communal dimension to it. The Easter Communion was an assertion of one's belonging to the Catholic community in which one lived: the whole local community was expected to go to Communion; not to have done so in the local communities of the time in which everyone knew everyone else would have been to stand out and be subject to suspicion by, if not exclusion from, the community. Even though this was a practice directly involving the individual, its context made it a very social and communal practice in which one affirmed and strengthened one's belonging to the community which itself was Catholic. It expressed one's Catholic identity.

Authors discuss the question as to whether Lateran IV's decree had as it aim to flush out members of the various heretical sects which arose in the thirteenth century from among genuine Catholics; they have different opinions on this question.[10]

A changed rite of penance

The ritual of penance throughout this period became simpler; it was reduced to those things which were seen to be central to the sacrament: the accurate telling of the penitent's sins and the priest's absolution. From the point of view of the rite, it was the latter which came to assume the greater importance and its form underwent significant change.

As mentioned in the previous chapter, when dealing with the thought of St Thomas Aquinas, throughout the first millennium and well into the twelfth century, the form in which reconciliation (or, to use later terminology, absolution) took place was deprecative or supplicatory, that is, it was in the form of a prayer or supplication for God's forgiveness. We find such a formula in the Gelasian Sacramentary: 'Lord God, who in the blood of your only Son has redeemed fallen man, give life to this penitent your servant, whose death you do not desire … heal his wounds'.[11] The reconciliation of the penitent was given expression in this prayer. It was the prayer of the Church, the body of Christ, which was presented to the Father on behalf of the penitent.

During the twelfth century another form of reconciliation or absolution came into use; it is the form to which we have become accustomed in recent Catholic history. It is called 'declarative': it is not in the form of a prayer for forgiveness but in the form of a declaration of forgiveness – thus the form 'I absolve you from all your sins in the name of the Father and of the Son and of the Holy Spirit'.

It was around the end of the twelfth century, at about the same time that the confession form of penance became dominant, when declarative forms of absolution emerged. Even then, the declarative or indicative formula was woven in with other formulae of deprecative style. St Thomas himself, who very much favoured the declarative formula, acknowledged that in his own time, it was not in common use.[12]

Each of these types of formulae – deprecative and declarative – fits into a different cast of thought regarding the sacrament of penance. The deprecative fits particularly well into the ecclesial, canonical form of ancient penance, and the indicative into the medieval and modern form of confession.

From contrition to absolution

We have spoken about a shift in the understanding of the sacrament of penance from one based on contrition to one based on absolution. This came about, as we have seen, at least in part because of some of the practical pastoral difficulties in using the sacrament.

A Franciscan friar and theologian, Duns Scotus (1265-1308), is significant in this transition. He was a Franciscan and so belonged to the milieu of the mendicant friars who eventually were to play so important a role as confessors of ordinary Catholics after the decree of Lateran IV. His theology of the sacrament of penance was different from that of St Thomas Aquinas on two points, each of which became very influential in the use of the sacrament among ordinary people in the centuries up to and after the Council of Trent and, indeed, remained influential into the first half of the twentieth century.

The first point was that, for Scotus, the essence of the sacrament was in the priest's absolution. The acts of the penitent (contrition, confession and satisfaction) were merely conditions necessary to receive the sacrament; they were not part of the essence of the sacrament.[13] Nevertheless the penitent's acts remained important. However, in the passing on and reception of this understanding of the sacrament among hard-working confessors and into minds that tended to simplify it, the fact that absolution was the essence of the sacrament meant that, in practice, the real importance of the sacrament tended to be seen as limited to the receiving of absolution.

Over the centuries, this brought about a use of the sacrament in which the penitent's part could be extremely minimal. It resulted in a commonly accepted practice in which a penitent would name some sin from the past so as to be able to receive the 'grace' of absolution. Penitents would re-confess sins for which they had already been absolved or else name sins that 'they must have committed' to receive 'the grace of absolution'; this took on the indefinite role of giving a grace not sufficiently related to the sins confessed. It was not conceived sufficiently well as being specifically the grace of the sacrament.

There were two problems in this I believe. First, the intrinsic link between penance as conversion, that is, as a part of the Christian way of life, and the use of the sacrament of penance was too easily lost. The sacrament of penance was reduced to but one of its dimensions, that of forgiveness. At its most extreme, this practice was barely the sacrament of penance; rather it became the sacrament of forgiveness! This reduction caused, and is still causing today, difficulty in seeing the purpose of the sacrament. In gospel terms, there is never any question of God's forgiveness; the question is rather our openness to the reception of that transforming forgiveness and the discovery of the obstacles in its path.

The second point upon which there was considerable theological difference between St Thomas Aquinas and Scotus was that Scotus conceived everything in terms of God's will, a way of seeing things called 'voluntarism'. This fitted into the growing temper of Scotus's age which, politically, was moving towards absolutism, a view of things in which everything depends upon the will of the ruler. Scotus, therefore, seeing God's will as dominant, conceived the sacrament of penance as ultimately an act of God's will to absolve the sinner and this found expression in the priest's absolution. This was in marked contrast to the approach of St Thomas in which God is at work bringing about the forgiveness of the sinner in the inner process of conversion (compunction and contrition) and which finds sacramental expression in the playing out of the sacrament between the penitent and the priest. Scotus's emphasis on God's will to forgive put the whole question in a very different context and promoted an understanding of the sacrament too concentrated on the legal or juridical analogy.

This was to bring future difficulties in its wake not just in the late Middle Ages but down to the twentieth and twenty-first centuries.

The Council of Trent

In response to the Protestant Reformation, the Council of Trent (1545-1563) acted to reform and renew the Catholic Church and to defend those of its doctrines and practices which were attacked by the Protestant Reformers. In regard to the sacrament of penance, among other things, Trent took up the idea behind the canon of Lateran IV requiring all Catholics to confess their sins annually at Easter; it saw in such a promotion of confession a means for the renewal of the life of the Church.

In 1551 the Council of Trent produced its doctrinal exposition on the sacrament of penance whose context was taken from the general teaching of the great medieval theologians without opting exclusively for one or other of their theologies. This material was approved by the council in the very short period of three days in late November of that year. It then produced fifteen canons on the sacrament over which it laboured at greater length.[14]

In these documents, the Council of Trent canonised the private form of the sacrament of penance which it received from the centuries immediately preceding it as if there had never been any other form of penance in the life of the Church. Andre Duval, historian of the Council of Trent suggests that the mentality of the council fathers – typical of their time – was so a-historical that they saw only the form they knew as ever having ever existed.[15]

The council speaks of this form of the sacrament as being of *jus divinum*, that is, it was not a creation of the Church, but had been given to the Church from the beginning by Christ. They simply identified this particular form of penance with the Church's power to forgive sins. In the post-Tridentine period this led to an excision of so much of the Catholic tradition of penance from the mind and practice of the Church. Historical evidence of other forms of penance tended to be read in terms of what Trent had canonised so that the form of private penance was read back into them. These were often seen as elaborations of the Tridentine model.[16]

The Council of Trent repeated Lateran IV's requirement of annual confession leading to Communion at Easter. Trent required that only mortal sin be confessed, that is, sin which would impede the Easter Communion. It encouraged people to confess all their sins and to do that more frequently than annually. It also states, as we saw in the previous chapter that, although it is of considerable value to confess venial sins, they need not be confessed since there are many other ways in which they can be forgiven.

In the period following the Council of Trent, there were important developments in the practice of the sacrament. First, it was in this period that the confessional was invented, its invention being attributed usually to St Charles Borromeo (1538-1584). Statistics from historians suggest that, by 1663, about twenty-eight per cent of parishes had confessionals and, by 1743, about eighty-eight per cent had them.[17] Their introduction by Charles Borromeo was initially more for the benefit of women than for men and so was probably aimed at diminishing any suspicions of sexual misconduct associated with the use of the sacrament. The confessional eventually became virtually universal and a symbol of the post-Tridentine Church. Its main purpose was to assure privacy during the celebration of the sacrament. At the height of the Catholic Reformation, confessionals became very significant and their position and decoration in churches was second only to the sanctuary used for Mass and for devotions to the reserved Eucharist. In new churches built after the eighteenth century, confessionals were a presumed part of a church building.

The second important development in the practice of the sacrament of penance in the post-Tridentine period concerned the various frequencies according to which Catholics used it. There were three rhythms of use according to Philippe Rouillard in his book on the sacrament: there was the annual rhythm of confession each Easter, which he suggests was quite enough for most people; there was a more frequent rhythm, perhaps monthly or even weekly for the devout; and, as we shall see, there was another, more variable rhythm, that of the parish missions, whose purpose was to renew the faith of a parish. A major purpose of these missions was to promote the making of a good confession by all parish members.[18]

Undoubtedly, the more frequent use of the sacrament was significant in establishing a different spirit in the post-Tridentine Church. Hsia, in his book on the world of the Catholic Renewal, suggests that the efforts of the council and the post-conciliar period were moderately successful. He suggests that in towns and villages near towns, the annual confession and Communion were moderately common by the middle of the seventeenth century, but that, by and large, such practice did not achieve the renewal it desired.[19] Delumeau suggests that priests and bishops came to the realisation that they could not ask too much of the greater part of their people and that it was necessary to come to terms with their 'spiritual' inertia and the lack of religious culture among them.[20]

By the middle of the eighteenth century, there was a growing tendency to refuse to fulfil the annual obligation and, in the nineteenth century, there was a strong and publicly expressed opposition to the practice of confession, especially among men.[21] Delumeau makes the interesting remark that after the French Revolution there were people who wanted to come back to Sunday Mass and to Easter Communion but would not come back to the use of confession, preferring, he says, to become distant from the Church.[22]

Rouillard's second rhythm of use of the sacrament was that among the devout members of the Church who celebrated the sacrament frequently. There were two types of practice of the sacrament among them, corresponding, roughly speaking, to the two approaches to the sacrament epitomised in the works of Scotus and Thomas Aquinas. The first approach was one where sins were confessed regularly but rather formally in order to gain the grace of absolution; the other was that which tended towards spiritual direction in which the penitent searched themselves in order to develop the process of conversion.

The third rhythm of the use of confession referred to by Rouillard is that of the parish missions. Parish missions began around the beginning of the seventeenth century and were a major innovation of the Catholic Renewal following the Council of Trent. They involved many new religious orders and similar groups: Jesuits, Capuchins, Vincentians, Theatines, Redemptorists, Passionists. One of the specific functions of these new orders was to conduct such parish missions. Groups of priests from them would go into parishes to conduct missions for a number of days or weeks, instructing the people and calling them to conversion and renewal, and leading them to make their confessions; these would be the culminating point of the mission.[23] Such missions played a large part in the renewal of the Church from the seventeenth to the twentieth centuries.

A fascinating phenomenon was that it became a fashion during the height of the Catholic Reformation in the seventeenth century to have a confessor and to put oneself forward as one of delicate and discerning, even scrupulous, conscience. Having a confessor was the done thing in the Catholic salons of France![24]

From the Council of Trent to at least the nineteenth century, there was a constant tension between emphasis on the seriousness of sin and conversion and emphasis on God's compassion and the ready availability of God's forgiveness. This was a return to the recurrent tension between rigour and laxity that is present in the history of penance and of moral theology in general.

There were saints who emphasised each of the poles of this tension. St Charles Borromeo emphasised the seriousness with which sin and conversion were to be taken and he had very wide influence in the whole Catholic world throughout the post-Tridentine period. On the other hand, there were saints, such as St Francis de Sales and St John Eudes, both of whom promoted a gentler approach in dealing with penitents: one based on the compassion and gentleness of God towards the sinner.[25]

From the middle of the seventeenth century, there arose a movement called 'Jansenism'. It took its name from Cornelius Jansen (1585-1634), a professor of theology in Louvain and eventually Bishop of Ypres in what is, today, Belgium. In 1640 he wrote a book called *Augustinus*. Five theses were drawn out of this book and condemned as heretical by the Roman authorities in 1653. What particularly was condemned in Jansen's book was a very pessimistic view of human nature which was seen as leading to the denial of free will in human beings, and, from that, to the denial that human beings could refuse grace and, in turn, from that, to the denial of the universality of the salvation gained by the death of Christ. This therefore involved the predestination of some to salvation and of others to condemnation.

Discussion continued among Jansenists and their opponents as to the accuracy of the Roman reading of Jansen's work. However, the important continuation of 'Jansenism' was not so much a strictly theological movement as an attitude and way of life within the Church. What is commonly referred to as 'Jansenism', or as 'Jansenistic', is a severe and demanding form of Catholicism with little tolerance for human weakness. This attitude was common from the seventeenth to the early twentieth centuries. Being founded on a rather negative view of human nature, it was wary of any laxity in the approach to sin and was unconvinced by talk of the primacy of God's love over human sinfulness. It set very demanding standards for the reception of Holy Communion. It required a high sense of worthiness and so promoted the necessity of confessing one's sins before reception. It discouraged frequent Communion.

The most significant opponents of Jansenism, both theologically and pastorally, were the Jesuits, whom Jansenists saw as presenting an easy-going and lax form of Catholicism which made too few demands upon sin-inclined human nature. They considered Jesuit attitudes to the sacrament of penance loose and irresponsible.

The twentieth century

The twentieth century had a very particular contribution to make to the history of the sacrament of penance. Pope Pius X published two decrees of relevance to this point: *Sacra Tridentina* of 1905 and *Quam Singulari* of 1910; these promoted frequent Communion and the admission of children to Communion at an earlier age.[26] Gradually, from the time these decrees were published, frequent and, eventually, weekly Communion became the normal custom for practising Catholics.

This had the effect of changing the practice of the sacrament of penance as well. Over the preceding centuries, the presumption had grown that one ought to confess all of one's sins in confession; along with that went another presumption that each time one went to Communion, one should go to confession beforehand. The effect of these presumptions was that a higher frequency of Communion brought with it a higher frequency of confession.

In the decades between Pius X's decrees and the middle of the twentieth century, a new pastoral practice meant that the Catholic people were urged to participate more and more frequently in Holy Communion. They were urged to practise Sunday Communion and to make a regular confession, perhaps on a monthly, perhaps on a weekly, basis. The placing of confession and Communion on different rhythms of time began to break the link that had previously existed between them. It remained necessary for anyone who had sinned seriously to confess their sins before receiving Communion.

This practice of regular confession from the 1940s to the 1970s brought larger numbers of Catholics to the sacrament of penance than had ever been the case in the entire history of the Church. Large numbers had been involved earlier in the annual Easter duty of confession, as they also were at times like Christmas, but there had never been such numbers on a weekly or monthly basis precisely because Catholics had never received Communion so frequently before. This is an important fact for us to consider in our deliberations on the sacrament today.

The Second Vatican Council

The comments made on the sacrament of penance in the documents of the Second Vatican Council are neither numerous nor extensive but they are significant as stimuli for the future theological development of the sacrament.

In the document on the Liturgy, we find the following statement: 'The rite and formulae of penance are to be revised so that they more clearly express both the nature and the effect of the sacrament.'[27] This simple statement points out the need for a new rite which gives better expression to the very nature of the sacrament. It implies that the previous rite did not express 'the nature and effect' of the sacrament sufficiently.

The document on the Church, *Lumen Gentium*, fills out a little more the nature and effect of the sacrament which was in need of clearer expression. It states:

> Those who approach the sacrament of penance obtain pardon from God's mercy for the offence committed against him, and are, at the same time, reconciled with the Church which they have wounded by their sins and which by charity, by example and by prayer labours for their conversion.[28]

This quotation opens up interesting dimensions of the sacrament. It links the forgiveness of God and reconciliation with the Church. It links the penitent and the Church not just by speaking of the wound which sin inflicts upon the Church but by speaking of the Church's working for the conversion of the sinner. This passage also opens up important perspectives for the future theological development of the sacrament and for the ritual with which it can be celebrated. It shows a greater awareness of the tradition regarding the sacrament than that of the post-Tridentine period.

The documents quoted above were published in 1963 and 1964. In 1973, the *Rite of Penance* was published as part of the Roman Ritual. This rite was produced in response to the request of Vatican II for a clearer expression of the nature and effect of the sacrament of penance.[29]

This *Rite of Penance* contains three rites: the *Rite for the Reconciliation of Individual Penitents* (commonly called the 'first rite'), the *Rite for Reconciliation of Several Penitents with Individual Confession and Absolution* (commonly called the 'second rite'), and the *Rite for Reconciliation of Several Penitents with General Confession and Absolution* (commonly called the 'third rite'). It was envisioned that the last of these three would be used only in restricted circumstances. Along with these three rites there is an Introduction of a theological nature which is a guide to the understanding of the nature of the sacrament of penance. It parallels similar documents appearing at the beginning of the rituals of all the rites revised according to the decrees of the Second Vatican Council. There are then further texts given for use in the various celebrations of the sacrament of penance, and three appendices. Appendix Two gives sample penitential services and perhaps, more importantly, the fifth part of the Introduction introduces these services in terms of their nature and structure, their benefit and importance.

At this point I will not deal with this document at length, save to note its importance as a document and to note two very important points of enrichment that have been written into all the rites: a much greater emphasis on the use of the word of God in the sacrament and a greatly enriched formula of absolution which expresses much more clearly the nature and effect of the sacrament of penance:

> God, the Father of mercies, through the death and resurrection of his Son has reconciled the world to himself and has sent the Holy Spirit among us for the forgiveness of sins; through the ministry of the Church may God give you pardon and peace, and I absolve you from your sins in the name of the Father, and of the Son, and of the Holy Spirit. Amen.

At this point we can conclude this treatment of the very varied history of the sacrament of penance and pass on to attempt to present salient theological and pastoral perspectives in the hope of stimulating its understanding and practice in the life of the Church.

Notes

1. Pierre-Marie Gy, 'Les bases de la pénitence moderne', *Maison Dieu* 117 (1974) 75.

2. Mary C. Mansfield, *The Humiliation of Sinners: Public penance in thirteenth century France* (Ithaca/ London: Cornell University Press, 1995) 52-3, 288-9; Jean Delumeau, *La confessione e il perdono* (Cibisello Balsamo [Milano]: Edizioni Paoline, 1992) 15-23; idem, *Sin and Fear: The emergence of a Western guilt culture, 13th-18th centuries* (New York: St Martin's Press, 1990) 198-205.

3. Delumeau, *La confessione*, 16.

4. ibid., 22.

5. ibid., 55-74.

6. ibid., 55-66.

7. ibid., 25-37.

8. Nicole Lemaître, 'Pratique et signification de la confession commaunitaire dans les paroisses au XVIe siècle', Groupe de la Bussière, ed., *Pratiques de la confession* (Paris: Cerf, 1983) 139-41.

9. Marcel Bernos, *Saint Charles Borromée et ses 'Instructions aux Confesseurs': Une lecture rigoriste par le clergé français (XVIe-XIXe siècle)* and Bernard Dompnier, *Misssions et Confession au XVIIe siècle*, Groupe de la Bussière, ed. Les Pratiques de la confession (Paris: Cerf, 1983) 185-223.

10. Pierre-Marie Gy, 'Le précepte de la confession annuelle (Latran IV, C. 21) et la détention des hérétiques', *Revue des Sciences philosophiques et theologiques* 58 (1974) 444-50; Thomas N. Tentler, 'The Summa for Confessors as an Instrument of Social Control', in C. Trinkhaus and H. Oberman, ed., *The Pursuit of Holiness in Late Medieval and Renaissance Religion*, Studies in Medieval and Renaissance Thought, X (Leiden, 1974) 103-37; Leonard Boyle, 'The Summa for Confessors as a Genre, and its Religious Intent', in C. Trinkaus and H. Oberman, ed., *The Pursuit ...*, 126-30.

11. 'Absolution (Formule de l')', in *Catholicisme* Vol. 1, cols 59-60.

12. ibid. See the article quoted from St Thomas Aquinas' *Summa Theologiae* in the above article of *Catholicisme*: S.T. III, q 84, art 3. Note Aquinas's rather qualified presentation of the indicative formula as *Convenientissima forma huius sacramenti* (final sentence of the *Respondeo dicendum* ...).

13. Jean Charles Payen, 'La pénitence dans le contexte culturel des XIIe et XIIIe siècles', *Revue des Sciences philosophiques et theologiques* 61 (1977) 421-2; Delumeau, *La confessione*, 51-3.

14. Andre Duval, *Des sacrements au Concile de Trente* (Paris: Cerf, 1985) 'La Confession', 151-208; Hubert Jedin, 'La nécessité de la confession privée selon le Concile de Trente', *Maison Dieu* 104 (1970) 88-115; Dionisio Borobbio, 'Le modele tridentin de la confession des péchés dans contexte historique', *Concilium* 210 (1987) 35-53.

15. Duval, *Des sacraments*, 185.

16. Thomas Aquinas is already interpreting the past tradition of the Church in terms of his preferred model of the sacrament in article 3 of question 84 of the third part of the *Summa*, quoted above.

17. R. Po-Chia Hsia, *The World of Catholic Renewal, 1540-1770* (Cambridge University Press, 1998) 198; John Bossy, 'The Social History of Confession in the Age of the Reformation', *Transactions of the Royal Historical Society*, 5th series, 25 (1975) 21-58; see 31-3.

18. Philippe Rouillard, *Histoire de la pénitence des origines à nos jours* (Paris: Cerf, 1996) 85-8.

19. Hsia, *The World*, 198-9.

20. Delumeau, *La confessione*, 49-66, esp. 56-7.

21. ibid., 151.

22. ibid., 151.

23. Rouillard, *Histoire de la pénitence*, 85-8; Dompnier, *Missions et confession*, 202-7; Hsia, *The World*, 200-1.

24. Delumeau, *La confessione*, 152.

25. Delumeau, ibid., 45-7; Bernos, *Saint Charles Borromée*, 185-200; Dompnier, *Missions et confession*, 221-2.

26. DS. Denzinger-Schonmetzer, *Enchiridion Symbolorum, Definitionum et Declarationum de rebus fidei et morum*. Editio XXXIII (Freiburg: Herder, 1965) nn. 1981-9 and 2137-44.

27. 'Constitution on the Sacred Liturgy' (*Sacrosanctum Concilium*) n. 72, in A. Flannery, ed., *Vatican Council II: The conciliar and postconciliar documents* (Dublin: Dominican Publications/ Newtown, NSW: E.J. Dwyer, 1987) 22.

28. 'Dogmatic Constitution on the Church' (*Lumen Gentium*) n. 11, in A. Flannery, ed., *Vatican Council II*, 362.

29. Sacred Congregation for Divine Worship, *The Roman Ritual. Rite of Penance, 1973.* (Sydney/ Wellington: E. J. Dwyer, 1975).

PART 2

Towards a Theology of
the Sacrament of Penance

Introduction

It is crucial that the biblical and theological enrichment which has come about in the life of the Church since the middle of the twentieth century make its presence felt in the renewal of the understanding and practice of the sacrament of penance. The renewal which has occurred in the understanding and use of the Scriptures and of the sacraments, along with the invigorated insights of christology and ecclesiology, need to have greater impact upon this sacrament. In this task we can find a stimulus in the General Introduction to the *Rite of Penance* published following the Second Vatican Council.[1]

To begin a presentation on this sacrament, Chapter Six will look at the understanding and use of the Scriptures which are crucial to the general renewal of the Church and, most especially, to the renewal of the sacrament of penance. Then Chapter Seven will look at that which stands at the heart of the entire Christian mystery and at the heart of the practical life of the Church: the death and resurrection of Jesus. The mystery of Christ's death and resurrection pulses through everything genuinely Christian. Chapter Eight will then look at conversion, sin and some specifics about the crisis and renewal of the sacrament of penance today.

We live in an age and a society which recognises itself less and less as Christian or at least minimises the meaning of 'Christian' to such an extent that the name can loose its distinctive meaning. At such a time it becomes even more important to grasp the distinctively Christian meaning of our faith and of its constitutive elements, such as the sacraments. For our present purpose, it becomes important to grasp the distinctively Christian meaning of the sacrament of penance, as we will see in Chapter Nine. The sacrament of penance is a Christian sacramental practice whose primary point of reference is the death and resurrection of Jesus; it belongs specifically and primarily to the sacramental dimension of the Church's life rather than to the moral dimension of that life, even though it involves that latter dimension.

In addition to this, any conception of the Church and its sacraments formed in the wash of the Second Vatican Council cannot ignore the Church's intrinsic and positive relationship to the whole of humankind. This is made clear in such central documents of Vatican II as those of the Constitutions on the Church and on the Church in the Contemporary World.[2] And so one cannot think about the sacrament of penance or practise it effectively now or in the future without this same intrinsic link to the rest of humankind: see Chapter Ten.

Notes

1. Sacred Congregation for Divine Worship. *The Roman Ritual. Rite of Penance* 1973 (Sydney/ Wellington: E. J. Dwyer, 1975) 4-19.

2. 'Dogmatic Constitution on the Church' of the Second Vatican Ecumenical Council, in A. Flannery, ed., *Vatican Council II: The conciliar and postconciliar documents* (Dublin: Dominican Publications/ Newtown, NSW: E. J. Dwyer, 1987) 350-451, nn. 1, 9, 48; 'Pastoral Constitution on the Church in the Contemporary World' of the Second Vatican Council, in A. Flannery, ed., ibid., 903-1001, nn. 1, 42, 45.

Chapter 6

The Scriptures, Memory and Penance

An essential element in any specifically Christian endeavour is the use of the Scriptures. In the light of the Church's rediscovery of their importance, reflected in the liturgical books of the Church, no sacrament is to be celebrated without their proclamation. Within Catholicism, the Scriptures have always been coupled with tradition, but the understanding of the relationship between tradition and the Scriptures has not always been clear. Scripture and tradition are not two independent realities alongside each other; rather, they are interdependent in their origin, use and development. The use of the Scriptures occurs within the living tradition which they enrich and strengthen. Our use of the Scriptures needs to be understood as occurring within that living tradition. It is a return to this basic Catholic principle which gives light to the use of the Scriptures. It avoids both fundamentalism and a rationalist reduction of the Scriptures to that which contemporary attitudes find acceptable.

Before dealing with the paschal mystery, which the sacrament of penance celebrates, we need to look at the importance of an understanding of the use of the Scriptures in the Christian life and, therefore, their importance in the celebration of the sacraments. Each sacrament, in its own specific way, gives body to the word of God proclaimed in the Scriptures. To paraphrase St Augustine's words: we bring the word of God to the elements used in the sacrament (e.g., bread and wine, water) and in the joining of word and elements, the sacrament comes about. The word of God takes form in each sacrament in accord with the sacramental elements upon which the sacrament is based. So, in Eucharist, the word is embodied in a meal and its core elements of bread and wine; in marriage, in the relationship of husband and wife, and so on for each sacrament. In each of the sacraments, the word is at work bringing us into communion with Christ in a specific way. Thus before we go on to ground the sacrament of penance in the paschal mystery, we need to consider the dynamics of the word of God in our lives and in our sacraments and the relation between the Scriptures and the Word of God.

To appreciate the importance of the Scriptures we need a renewed sense of their role in the Christian life. They are not only about the past nor are they merely a source of truths to be believed or morals to be lived. They are a means of encountering Christ present to us now as he was to the two disciples on the road to Emmaus.[1]

In the first instance, this encounter occurs simply because we listen to the Scriptures or we read them, and listening and reading are interactive activities. Whenever we listen to or read a book, an article, a poem or even just a few words, we interact with what we hear or read. This is not just a matter of absorbing some words but of setting up an interaction between these words, this text, and what is already in our minds and hearts.

Looking at this from another angle, when I read, I am being invited by the text and the author behind it to take up a new way of seeing things or maybe to see something for the first time. I am being invited to allow the view of the author to pass over into my mind and so to look at the matter being considered from that new point of view. I allow a certain merging of perspectives to occur between my own and the author's and I come away enriched by that interaction, that passing-over, that merging with the author's point of view. My world is enriched and extended by this interaction. Even in the instance in which I disagree with the perspective of the text or author I am reading, an enrichment in fact still occurs in that very disagreement. Even when I cannot take in what I read the same point is made: it is because I do not already have in my mind the wherewithal to let the new words or text come to me. In such a case there is not enough in common between myself and the text to allow an interaction to take place.

Reading or listening are human activities and reading or listening to the Scriptures is a human activity; it has the same character as any other act of human reading. This is an important point if we are to understand why and how we use the Scriptures in the living of our faith, in its further penetration into us and its theological development.

Reading the Scriptures is an interaction between the text or author and the reader. This is what happens when we read. The fundamentalist approach to the Scriptures, which sees them as the unmediated word of God, is an illusion. It presumes that the words of the Scriptures come to us directly from God; it sees the human author as having as little effect on the text as a telephone line has on the words of a caller. Such an approach has the consequent danger that the person identifies what they hear or read with the unmediated words of God. Their own interpretation of them then becomes the word of God.

But to read or listen to the Scriptures is to allow a dialogue to take place in us which is parallel to the dialogue narrated in the scriptural passage. It allows us to be invited by God to see the world in a particular way. The scriptural passage is the catalyst which allows there to occur in us, within our circumstances and our moment of history, what occurred in the circumstances and moment of history of the passage we hear or read.

What is specific about the reading of the Scriptures is that they have a specific character as writings. This specific nature consists in their presenting to us in writing the unveiling of God which has occurred throughout the

Jewish and Christian history of revelation. These writings are accepted by those belonging to the Christian tradition as the normative writings narrating the workings of God among his people. And they are seen as inspired because in them the Spirit reproduces in each age in a new situation what occurred in that past event narrated in the Scriptures. For Christians, the history of that revelation reached its unsurpassable climax with the person, life, death and resurrection of Jesus, in whom God is revealed in our flesh.

Listening to or reading the Scriptures is in itself an act of conversion. In reading them we enter into the point of view or perspective that they offer us, thus entering into an act of conversion. The Scriptures tell us that Jesus calls those around him to conversion and the word used for that in the Greek is *metanoia*, which means 'to go beyond our mind', that is, to allow what he says and does to take us beyond where we are. Thus it involves a change of mind, of perspective or point of view. So our very reading of the Scriptures puts us in the way of conversion to the perspective or point of view which has emerged in our tradition of communication and communion with God.

As Jesus, the Word of God in our flesh, spoke in his own time, so he speaks again now in the echo which occurs in our present time when the Scriptures, the written embodiment of the word of God, are proclaimed. Christ is present among us now in the proclamation of the word.[2]

The Scriptures and memorial

For our purpose here, we need to understand how these writings pass the word of God on to us. They do this within the ongoing tradition or handing on of the Christian faith and we can shed further light on that by means of the concept of memorial. We are accustomed to using this concept in the theology of the Eucharist but it is also critical for our theological understanding of the Scriptures and of each of the sacraments.

Memory and remembering in the literature and practices of Israel involve a very dynamic conception of the relationship between the past, the present and the future. There is a dynamism intrinsic to their relationship which is crucial to Israel's understanding of God and the meaning of God's revelation. When Israel remembers the Exodus, it is not a matter of mental recall, but of drawing their present experience of life into alignment with that founding event of their life and relationship with God. When the prophets urge Israel at the time of their exile in Babylon to remember their exodus out of slavery in Egypt, they are urging them to draw these two events into alignment, thus to discover the continuity between them: the liberating activity of God.

Israel aligns its present experience with the Exodus because, in that crucial event of their past, they discovered who God is: the One who has revealed himself as their deliverer out of slavery. In the midst of their experience of exile in Babylon, they are invited to align that experience of exile with their past experience of slavery in Egypt and so with God's delivery of them out of that slavery. They are invited to expect God to deliver them now out of Babylonian exile just as he had delivered them out of their Egyptian slavery.

The God they discovered in the Exodus is the God with whom they are always in living communion. It is the same God who was with them in their escape from slavery in Egypt who is with them at every moment of their history and in their individual lives. They recognise him now and hence know what to expect of him from that reference to the past event of the Exodus, in which he had shown them what he is like and what to expect of him. The great events of the past were not just past events but portents of what God would continue to offer them in every generation of his people's history; they are portents of what is available to them in their constant relationship with God. He was, is and ever will be the same God who has shown himself in the Exodus.

Similarly, the people of Israel keep God's commandments in memory of the Exodus. That is, in obeying these words of God they will find themselves set free by God, set free from the slavery in which ignoring one's parents, worshipping other gods, or allowing murder or adultery would ensnare them. Keeping the commandments is a way of meeting the God of the Exodus, the One who sets free.

This 'memorial' dynamic is at the heart of the New Testament. When we read the Gospels, especially, we are placing ourselves within that same dynamic. We are placing our lives before God in memory of Christ's death and resurrection. As we allow ourselves to pass over in mind and action into an alignment with Jesus, we are placing ourselves before God, who will respond to us as he responded to Jesus. Constantly we are invited to draw our lives in their current circumstances into alignment with Jesus in his life, death and resurrection.

The Father raised Jesus out of death into life. This is the New Testament Exodus. In this Passover, the Father overcomes those things which stand between us and himself who is our source of life. We are invited into this Passover now as we encounter in the Word proclaimed, in the Eucharist and in the other sacraments (each in their own way) this same God doing what he did in Jesus, drawing us out of life destined to death into life with God who is the very source of all life.

Once the Resurrection was revealed and grasped by the disciples, they proclaimed the whole life of Jesus in the light of that resurrection out of death since only then did they properly understand his life. Only then did they see that the God active in the Exodus had now extended himself in this new Exodus out of death, this new Passover out of slavery and death into freedom and life.

Every word and action of Jesus took on new light for the first disciples after he was raised from death and they presented his words and actions to their hearers, and eventually to their readers, as the words and actions of the risen Lord. These are enshrined in our four Gospels.

Thus it is that when we read the New Testament, we are caught up in this relationship between past, present and future. What Jesus was doing and what God was doing in and through his servant and Son, Jesus, was done for us and is to be done in us. Jesus who heals the blind is now at work healing our blindness; Jesus who forgives the sinner is now at work forgiving our sin. When we, like the blind man, call out 'Lord, that I may see', we place ourselves and our blindness before the One who comes to give the blind sight. In this, we seek to tap into the working of God among us in accord with the memorial dynamic which flows through the whole of God's working among human beings as that is recounted in the Scriptures. In this way the healing power of Jesus, once shown in his healing miracles and his forgiveness of sinners, penetrates into the areas of estrangement from God that are in us, as the blindness of the blind man acted as an estrangement from God in him. In the blindness of the blind, Jesus touched human malaise and brought to it the power of the kingdom of God; so he does now, as we align ourselves with the blind man to discover the human malaise in us and allow it to be touched by the power of his kingdom.

As we approach the person, life, death and resurrection of Jesus presented to us in the Gospels, we go through a process of reading as described above. We are caught up in the memorial dynamic so that what happened in him and his situation might be drawn into alignment with us and what happens in us and our situation. In this way, we may see patterns of similarity and dissimilarity emerge between him and us, his situation and our situation. This can apply to our lives individually, to our lives in society and to our life as a society. We can allow a certain merging to take place between Jesus and his attitudes and perspectives in given situations and encounters, on the one hand, and our own parallel situations and encounters, on the other.

In this way, his life and words and works penetrate into our lives and words and works and we see ourselves in his light; and in his light, we come to stand before the living God. In this is judgment, the call to repentance, conversion, forgiveness, gracious love and glory.

In speaking of the Scriptures as inspired, we are saying that they prove to be the means by which the Holy Spirit of God brings us to this encounter with Jesus the Christ and through and with him, into encounter with the Father. The Scriptures have shown themselves to be a means by which the first disciples' original experience of Jesus is brought to Christians of every generation. The Spirit of God has been found breathing in the Scriptures expanding into all times and places the gift of Pentecost.

This consideration of the Scriptures has been important for two reasons: first, as the basis of the presentation of the paschal mystery of Jesus' death and resurrection, which we will present in the next chapter and, secondly, for the Christian understanding of forgiveness, conversion and sin contained in significant gospel narratives. The sacrament of penance is the sacramental embodiment and celebration of these narratives. It finds its substance in the celebration of what is narrated in the Scriptures with regard to forgiveness, conversion and sin. The sacrament is there to bring these narratives into effect in the present for the forgiven sinner in need of conversion. We will come back to the importance of the Scriptures in the final chapter of this book in order to speak of their role in the renewal of the sacrament today.

Notes

1. There are many works that could be referred to here. I would like to draw the reader's attention particularly to a recent document of the English and Scottish Episcopal conferences: Catholic Bishops' Conference of England and Wales/ Catholic Bishops' Conference of Scotland, *The Gift of Scripture* (London: The Catholic Truth Society, 2005).

2. *General Instruction of the Roman Missal*, third typical ed. (Washington DC: United States Conference of Catholic Bishops, 2003) Liturgy Documentary Series 2, nn. 27, 29, 60.

Chapter 7

The Death and Resurrection of Jesus and the Sacrament of Penance

In the previous chapter we began to look at the fundamental biblical approach to dealings between human beings and God called 'memorial'. It is the dynamic by which faith in God is handed on. Before elaborating on its working within the biblical and Christian tradition, we need to note that this memorial dynamic is not something purely biblical or Christian. It is a part of being human which finds accentuated expression in the biblical tradition.

We can see memorial at work in our relationship to our parents, for instance. We live in memory of them, that is, we live out of them, we live 'from' them not just physically but personally and culturally. We live out of the inheritance we receive from them and we live it out: we extend it, we carry it forward. We come to a stage in our lives in which we accept as our own what we have received from them and, at the same time, distinguish ourselves from what we have received from them, thus modifying our inheritance from them and affirming our difference from them within the ongoing tradition of continuity in difference. This living out of them and living them out is not a choice; it is part of being a human being at a preconscious, unreflected yet experiential, level. It is only gradually, and through developing personal experience, that we realise the profound and inevitable link between us and what has gone before us. This inheritance from the past shapes our direction into the future. This handing on is at work on a larger and a smaller scale. On the larger scale, our parents are handing on to us the culture and tradition of which they and we are part; and on the smaller scale, they are handing on to us our personal lives in a relationship between them and us.

We can also see the memorial dynamic at work at times of emotional or psychological difficulty. At such times, we have to seek what there is in our past which blocks us from moving ahead. Dealing with the past can set us free in the present. This is the human memory at work. All of this occurs within that dynamic which we have described as 'living out of and living out' our past. It is simply a dimension of human nature.

The history of events in which God has been revealed to us have been events in the history recorded in the Old and New Testaments and so is caught up in the memorial dynamic of the human beings involved. This history of events involving the revelation of God brings to greater awareness the essentially historical character of human beings through the dynamic of memory.

We now want to look at the memorial dynamic as it applies to Jesus' death and resurrection. As part of the Jewish people, Jesus and his disciples lived within a tradition based on memory: the dynamic relationship of past, present and future described above. This was the mindset at work in the people, its institutions and its relationship with God. This was expressed in its life of prayer, as that was practised in the Temple, the synagogue and the home.

The first Christians used images from the Old Testament, such as 'the lamb of God', 'the Passover', 'redemption from slavery', 'sacrifice', and placed them alongside the death and resurrection of Jesus as a means of going beyond what the eye sees and the ear hears to discover what God was doing in Jesus. These were used to 'see into' his life, death and resurrection. They provided the means of going beyond appearances to discover the deeper dimension of what was going on within the ongoing tradition of God's dealings with his people. Thus in the narrative of the two disciples on the road to Emmaus, Jesus takes them through the Scriptures, beginning with Moses and the prophets, in order to lead them to the discovery of himself as the one sent by God (Luke 24:13-35). This pattern of taking the disconcerted disciples through the Scriptures to bring them to the discovery of Jesus recurs in the New Testament writings. It was by means of seeing his death and resurrection within the memorial tradition of Israel that they discovered Jesus and what God was doing in him.

In the life, death and resurrection of Jesus, there are two levels of thought of which we need to be aware: the first concerns the happenings in the course of his life, his death and his disciples' reported experience of him alive after his death; the second concerns the discovery of the meaning of these happenings within the memorial tradition of the biblical revelation. This second level is that of revelation, where those given the gift of the Spirit are enabled to discern in the events concerned a new stage in the revelation of the God who had been revealing himself throughout Israel's history.

The life and death of Jesus were events like any other events in human life, and the discovery of the empty tomb and the report of the disciples that they had discovered Jesus alive after his death are events like other human events, even though the resurrection had never before been revealed. It was seeing those events in the light of the biblical tradition which enabled them to be seen as revealing and redeeming events.

The disciples after Jesus' death are disillusioned and cast down on seeing what had been 'their own hopes' dashed (Luke 24:21-24). All of them, like the two disciples on the road to Emmaus, had to learn to read this event aright within Israel's memorial tradition. In the narratives of the appearances of Jesus after the resurrection, there is confusion and a lack of understanding among his disciples. On the one hand, they had to return to the heart of their own tradition as people of the Scriptures in order to see Jesus rightly; and on the other hand, they had to learn to read that tradition in a new way, that of seeing his death and resurrection as the latest and the definitive moment of that tradition.

Once this merging of Jesus' death and resurrection and their own memorial tradition occurred, things began to fall into place. Their memorial expectation was that the God of the Exodus would keep liberating them from slavery, that he would keep meeting them in the ongoing history of their people and that he would do in new circumstances the liberating he had done in the Exodus. Thus the Father's raising Jesus out of death is the action of the same God of the Exodus extending himself in this new Exodus in which the ultimate enemies are overcome – death and the evil which stalks our human life and world.

Once the disciples had overcome their foreshortened expectations by which they had limited their understanding of what God would do, they could see the God of the Exodus at work still, anew and supremely.

They then extended this insight throughout the whole of their presentation of Jesus, of his life and ministry in the Gospels, since they proclaim the life of Jesus and the events occurring within it as events within the memorial tradition of Israel. In this way, the Gospels are ever conscious that the acts and words of Jesus are intrinsically related to the Old Testament, memorially related to the Old Testament, we may say. The whole of the gospel tradition is aware that the one who acted in the Old Testament was now acting in the person of Jesus.

We receive these narratives of the Gospels as our means of seeing into our lives and of discovering here and now the One who spoke and acted then. We believe in Jesus' resurrection out of death as our way of knowing what to expect of God now and in the future.

The death and resurrection of Jesus as redeeming event

The account of the death and resurrection of Jesus dominates the four Gospels not just in the proportion of the text which they comprise but in the orientation of each account and in their anticipation of that death and resurrection in the very recounting of the words and events of the life of Jesus.

Coming to faith in Jesus risen out of death is the beginning of Christianity and the source of its constant recurrence in each successive generation. This is a matter of faith, of the recognition in faith of Jesus alive after death as the first disciples recognised him in the appearances in the Upper Room (John 20:19-29), on the road to Emmaus (Luke 24:13-35), on the lake side (John 21:4-8), as Magdalen recognised him in the garden (John 20:11-18) and as Paul recognised him on the road to Damascus (Acts 9). Paul of course was born 'out of due season', rather like ourselves and all later believers. This discovery of the living Christ is not just a discovery of the first disciples but ours, that is, it belongs to all of us who have not seen him but who believe in him (John 20:29). This discovery has occurred through all the generations from that of the first disciples to our own. When we speak of Jesus' death and resurrection in this context our concern is with this continuing Christian discovery that the One who died on the cross 'under Pontius Pilate' is indeed alive and gives us life.

To proceed with the development of an understanding of the sacrament of penance we will enter into dialogue with the faith of the first disciples as that is presented in the Gospels. This dialogue or interaction will seek to bring into alignment the faith presented in the Gospels and our faith as contemporary believers. What follows is an example of the process of reading the Scriptures described in the previous chapter. We seek to find in those once and forever revealing events which occurred in the life of Jesus his continuing revelation in our time and circumstances.

Paschal

Jesus' death and resurrection was and is understood in several ways which tap into the imagery, expectations and practices of the Jewish people of whom he was one and without whose religious life we would not be able to understand him. This understanding flows from the dynamic of memorial.

Among the many ways used to understand Jesus' death and resurrection was that of the Exodus and its celebration, the feast of the Passover. This event was the founding event of the nation and religion of Israel just as the death and resurrection of Jesus is the founding event of Christianity. The prominence of the feast of Passover and its association with Jesus is very evident in the New Testament texts.

As outlined above in the introduction to this part of the book on the theology of the sacrament of penance, the alignment of Jesus' death and resurrection with the feast of the Passover leads to the use of the term 'paschal mystery' to describe them. As Israel passed from slavery in Egypt through the Red Sea and journeyed in the wilderness to the land of promise; so Jesus passes from human life as we know it through death into the life of promise with the Father, which is true human life. The description of Jesus' death and resurrection as paschal mystery emphasises that his whole life was a movement through his death into the resurrection and return to the Father with whom he becomes the source of the Spirit and the risen life for us. That Spirit among us takes us through that same Passover into life through, with and in Jesus.

Mystery

By the word 'mystery' in this context, we mean a reality which, upon our experiencing it, we find to contain more than we expected, to have depth to it beyond its appearances, to contain more than the eye can see or the ear can hear.

A mystery in this sense is at work when a supporter goes to a football match. He or she watches the players doing certain things in a skilled manner in obedience to the ritual patterns required of them. But the supporter gets involved beyond the logic of the appearances. This is so because a football match is a mystery in the sacramental or liturgical sense of the word. The game in its ritual triggers something in the supporters which carries them way beyond any proportionate response to the skills and patterns obvious in the game into depths not easy to describe but which we can speak of as their sense of identification with one or other of the teams at play. This sense of identity fuels their participative energy. Such a game is what we mean by a mystery in the sacramental sense of the word. As the football match functions for the supporters, so the sacraments function for the believer in Christ's death and resurrection with regard to that death and resurrection. They are a mystery revealing that death and resurrection and offering participation in them.

Following these introductory thoughts let us now look at the mystery of Jesus' life, death and resurrection in more detail. It is itself a mystery because in that individual life we discover the significance of our own and every other human life.

Jesus' life and death

Looking at the course of the life of Jesus as that is presented in any of the Gospels we find that conflict very quickly arises and that this conflict builds up to his death. If we count the repetitions of the conflict stories in each of the Gospels, we will find over ninety of them. These narratives are extremely important in the playing out of the human forces involved in the life of Jesus. For our theological purposes in this book, I would like to look at these conflicts in terms of four groups with whom Jesus is engaged in conflict, namely: the people, the religious leaders, his own disciples, and Pontius

Pilate. In none of Jesus' conflicts with these various people are we dealing with situations so simplistic that we can reduce them to a matter of 'goodies versus baddies'. These conflicts have within them all the subtlety, ambiguity and blindness which are part of the conflicts which arise in all human lives and societies.

In the conflict of Jesus with the *people* (e.g., Mark 6:1-6; Matt 13:54-58; Luke 4:16-30; Matt 11:16-19; Luke 7:31-35; John 6:22-33), the people try to foist onto him their own ideas about what the Messiah should be like. In their first century situation, this would have been framed by the conquest of Palestine by the Romans, the ensuing oppression of the people and the many consequent insurrections among them. The Roman conquest aroused expectations among the people that God would raise up a deliverer for them, thus the coming of Jesus among them was seen in that light. Many of the people's favoured Old Testament prophetic texts encouraged the expectation of a kingly and warrior-like Messiah associated with the promise of the re-establishment of a Davidic kingdom.

Jesus' proclamation of the kingdom of God, even accompanied as it was with a call for conversion (Mark 1:14-15; Matt 4:12-17), was heard by the people in terms of their experience of oppression and their own expectations. The difference between their understanding of the kingdom of God and that of Jesus was what was at stake in many of these conflict narratives. And underlying all of this was a fundamental human and religious attitude which was at work then, is now and will always be at work among human beings. This attitude sees God as serving our human purposes. The people try to foist onto Jesus what they think the kingdom should be about and therefore what Jesus should be doing and bringing about among them. The people seek 'cheap religion', one which is governed and shaped by their needs and desires. In this spirit they wanted to make of Jesus a miracle-worker and a 'king', whereas his miracles occurred only as a response to faith and he fled their attempts to make him king. The foisting onto Jesus of their expectations and Jesus' refusal to fulfil them led to their rejection of him. They were dominated, as we all are, by their desires and by their own way of seeing things to such an extent that they were blind to what he was presenting to them (cf. Mark 4:10-12; Matt 13:10-15; Luke 8:9-10).

All the temptations that the people offered Jesus to go aside from the path that he saw to be his are presented in the narratives of the Temptations in the Desert (Mark 1:12-13; Matt 4:1-11; Luke 4:1-13). These narratives are placed at the beginning of each of the Synoptic Gospels. It is in these narratives of Jesus in the desert being tempted by Satan that we see Jesus choosing and clarifying his 'way' as that came to him from the Father. The Satan puts other things to him, all of them involving the debasement of God for human purposes: the cheap religion of turning stones into bread, of worshipping power and glory, of presuming on God and putting God to the test, rather than entrusting oneself to God. These temptations in the wilderness are the same temptations put to Jesus during his lifetime to go ways other than that which springs from his relationship to the Father. Notice that all of these conflicts are about God and what God is like.

Jesus' constant conflict with the *religious leaders* of the people, as presented in the Gospels, is also about God (cf. Mark 2:18-22; 2:23-28; 3:1-6; 3:22-30; 7:1-23; 8:11-21; and 11:27-33 and their parallels in Matthew and Luke). Ostensibly these conflicts are about food laws or the Sabbath or Jesus' authority but they really come down to different understandings about God and God's concerns. For Jesus, the healing of a human being is more important to God than what you do or not do on the Sabbath; likewise Jesus presents a God who desires to save the adulterous woman, not to see her stoned to death. For Jesus' opponents, God's concerns are about law and its detail, about ritual purity, about the Sabbath. In these conflicts we see the constant temptation of those who are religious to reduce God to less than he is, to limit God to our human institutions and our human imagination.

Jesus has frequent conflicts with his own *disciples*. Their attitudes and expectations are very close to those of the people. James and John seek the first seats in his kingdom (Mark 10:35-40; Matt 20:20-23). After Peter's profession of faith Jesus goes on to speak about his death and resurrection and Peter rebukes him for thinking like that. To this, Jesus responds: 'Get behind me Satan, you think not as God thinks but as men think' (cf. Mark 8:31-38; Matt 16:24-28; Luke 9:22-27). Here we have a reminiscence of the Temptations narratives. The disciples do not understand the way of Jesus until after his death and resurrection. There is a gap between what Jesus is saying and what human beings are able to hear. The enthusiasm of his disciples is an enthusiasm dominated by their own expectations; the noise of their own desires blocks out the settling of his word into them.

As Jesus is betrayed, arrested and put on trial, the enmities behind these conflicts come to a head. He is led to *Pontius Pilate*, who holds power over life and death. All that has built up over the years of his ministry climaxes as he is brought before the person who has responsibility for law and order and the governance of the people. In the encounter between Jesus and Pilate – the underside of which is so well brought out in John's Gospel – we have an encounter between the power of this world, and all that surrounds and motivates it, and the power which has come into the world in Jesus.

Pilate has the choice of serving his own ambitions and political ends or of doing justice. He has political pressure put on him by those around him: '... if you do not condemn this man you are no friend of Caesar' (cf. John 19:12). What is presented to us in the Gospels is the political pressure and manoeuvring that we know in our own society and any other human society. Jesus is the victim of these political machinations, he is the victim of Pilate's desire for the furtherance of his career, he is the victim of the compromise in which the Jewish leaders find themselves with the Roman authorities. He is the victim of the human preference for ambition and political compromise over justice.

There is also a broader dimension to all these conflicts. Jesus' society is one in which Rome, the imperial power, has conquered his native land: a situation replicated in so much of human history. The same effects occurred in that situation which we see occurring in other similar situations: there was oppression, there were attempts to free the conquered people by violence, there were collaborators, and suspicion and mistrust were widespread. Such things colour the entire social and political scene. Jesus could not carry out his mission from the Father outside the situation in which he lived. People could not hear what he had to say and see what he did outside that situation and so he was interpreted within it. Whatever he said, he was seen by all sides in terms of that social and political situation. Thus, like many before and after him, he was a victim of the situation in which he lived.

Similarly, Jesus was a victim of the jockeying for position which was so much a part of the career paths of aspiring leaders in the Roman Empire. Pilate could be coerced by people who had the potential to threaten or strengthen his position within this career structure. Jesus' fate is shaped by Pilate's very participation in that worldwide desire for prominence and profit.

Jesus' death comes about because of the way human beings are: because of our slavery to our needs and desires, because of our fickleness, because of our blindness, because we are caught up in a social atmosphere which shapes and determines our way of seeing things and our actions. We are subject to so many forces which shape and control us consciously and unconsciously. Our humanity is distorted and frustrated by such forces. This is a slavery: it impedes us, makes us unfree, and makes us blind to what is for our own good.

This negative dimension of human life is called 'sin' in the biblical tradition; it is a sinfulness which pervades our human situation which we in turn re-enforce by expressing it in our actions and decisions. What we see at work in the life of Jesus and in the conflicts which lead up to his death is this human reality bearing in on him. He is caught by it and in his death suffers its effects; it brings about his death; it kills Jesus the Christ. The sin which kills him does not just occur in his own time: we have seen that those things which lead to his death are part of the same human reality which was at work before him and is at work after him. It is the human sinfulness which is part of the human condition of all of us which brought him to his death. It is this continuing reality which has the same effect on him as it does on others. His voluntary subjection to it is part of his solidarity with us. In the face of this reality, Jesus makes choices grounded in his relationship with the Father. We see this played out in the Temptations and in the Agony in Gethsemane. He holds to the Father and the Father's ways to such an extent that they became transparent in him. He is the perfect image of the God we cannot see.

In him, and in the conflicts in which he is engaged, we have revealed to us the ways of God and the ways of human beings as they contrast with the ways of God. These conflicts reveal the very features of God and the way of God in the human actions, words and attitudes of Jesus, as they reveal the features of the sinful ways of human beings. The conflicts are important because they reveal the contrasts between God and human beings and in that contrast we can see human sinfulness over against the holiness of God in Jesus.

Resurrection out of death

The Father takes the death imposed on Jesus by human beings and turns it into the way to life beyond measure.

The discovery of Jesus alive after death and alive beyond death by the Christian community is their discovery of his being raised out of death by the Father. This resurrection out of the death imposed upon him by human beings is the Father's vindication of Jesus. It is the Father's confirmation of the way of Jesus over against the 'ways' of those who brought him to his death. It is the Father's putting into effect the words said over Jesus at his baptism (Mark 1:9-11; Matt 3:13-17; Luke 3:21-22) and at his Transfiguration (Mark 9:2-10; Matt 17:1-9; Luke 9:28-36): 'This is my Son, the beloved, my favour rests on him'. The resurrection reveals that Jesus' way is God's way.

The resurrection is Jesus' entry into life in God which is the future of our life. It is the glorification of Jesus in his humanity and his manifestation as Word of God, that is, as the expression of God's very self in our human flesh and history. In this the Passover is completed. Jesus passes from this world to the Father; he passes from human life as we know it, subject to the power of evil and death, to human life as God intends it to be – a communion of life and love with him, a Passover into that way of being human with Jesus of which he is 'the way, the truth and the life'.

Made Sin for Us

Looking back over the mystery of Jesus' death and resurrection with an eye to the sacrament of penance, Paul's phrase that Jesus 'was made sin for us' (2 Cor 5:21) gives us a rich and powerful direction to follow. It is a true and striking phrase. When we look at the process of Jesus' condemnation, it involves the policing, legal and judicial arms of the society of his time. These are the means by which human societies deal with those they consider destructive to their society, those who are called 'criminals'. Criminals are those whom every society isolates as incompatible with its well-being. They are a threat. Criminals are the 'sinners' of human society. They are those who have strayed into ways that a society cannot allow to continue because they put that society at risk. They are those whom society excludes either permanently or temporarily by means of some structure of exclusion.

This is how the society of Jesus' time dealt with him. It identified him as one who could not be allowed to continue because he posed a threat to it. The various officials and the populace in general saw him as a fraud, a rebel, a blasphemer. He needed to be dealt with. Human society did in Jesus' regard what it does in regard to all whom it considers criminals or 'sinners': it used the force of law to exclude him from society. The death penalty was imposed on him. Thus in the very dynamics of the working out of his life, he is treated as 'sinner', he becomes 'sinner' for us. In a juridic, societal sense, Jesus becomes a 'sinner', a criminal.

In yet another, theological, sense, Jesus becomes sin for us. Biblically, his cry on the cross, 'My God, my God, why have you abandoned me?', is the cry appropriate to the sinner because the sinner is the one cut off from God, abandoned by God because the sinner in their sin has cut their ties to God. God promises to be faithful to those who follow his ways and keep his covenant; but on the cross we have the faithful Jesus crying out with the cry of the sinner, those whose actions and attitude of heart bring about separation from God, the living One and Giver of life. In this separation we see the link between sin and death as the Scriptures see it: sin is separation from God, the Giver of life.

In his experience of abandonment by God, therefore, Jesus becomes sin for us, he enters into the ultimate experience that sin brings upon human beings. Not only has he lived our human life from beginning to end but he has fulfilled his solidarity with us in our sinful situation, having initiated such solidarity in his reception of baptism from John the Baptist, a baptism of repentance undertaken by sinners.

Jesus' becoming what we are in order to enable us to become what he is, is the wonderful exchange which so fired the imagination of the Fathers of the Church: here is the one who is the perfect image of the God we cannot see and who takes on everything that is ours, including the sinfulness that pervades our lives. He does this in order that we may pass-over into the life God intends for us. Here is the one who has come to give himself as a ransom for us who are enslaved to evil and death. He, in his unbreakable relationship to the Father, enters into death and into the ultimate experience of sin (abandonment by God) in order that his relationship to the living Father – stronger than the powers of separation (sin and death) – may deliver us by its power from those powers.

Jesus' relationship to the Father – expressed in Luke's words of Jesus on the cross: 'Into your hands, I commend my spirit' (Luke 23:46) – is stronger than the power of death to extinguish our life and stronger than the power of sin to separate us from God. Jesus' relationship to the Father, the living One, holds firm even in the experience of abandonment, even in the face of death. He keeps alive within our humanity – in his own self – that relationship to God which is the source of our life, and he does this even in the experience of abandonment and death. In him life wrestles with death and with the abandonment and isolation brought about by sin; and, in him, life wins. Our life's source, God, is kept within our human world in Jesus. From Jesus will pour forth upon all humanity, streams of life-giving water, the Spirit. In his communion with the Father at the cost of his own life and at the cost of the experience of abandonment, we are ransomed from the powers that would put us to death. He dies to put to death the powers that are in human beings which in their turn had put him to death. He dies for those who kill him.

This is the revelation of God to us. In this we are ransomed from slavery to death and sin. Jesus is the perfect image of the God we cannot see; in him we see who God truly is and what God wants for us and how he stands in regard to us, even in our sinfulness. Here we encounter the God who dies for us while we are yet sinners.

The sacrament of penance embodies this wonderful mystery, and its celebration needs to occur within its aura.

In the resurrection the Father vindicates Jesus, he 'takes the side of' Jesus, thus indicating where he, the Father, stands in the conflicts which led to Jesus' death. He stands with Jesus, and continues to call him his beloved Son. There is a reversal at work here. The one whom human society names 'sinner' is named 'holy' by God and so the human decisions and attitudes and situation which led to his death are shown to be 'sinful'. In this contrast between the actions of human beings and the dynamic behind them, on the one hand, and the action of God, on the other, the light of God falls upon those human actions and that human situation to show where evil is at work in them, and where good.

In principle this is not just a matter pertaining to the individual life of Jesus alone because the whole drama of human life and its relationship to God is played out in Jesus' life. Whenever we find elsewhere in human life and history the sort of actions and the sort of situation that we find in the life of Jesus, these situations fall under the same judgment of God shown in the resurrection of Jesus from the dead.

The Father's response to humanity in the resurrection of Jesus, however, was not to replicate humanity's rejection of Jesus but, rather, to return the risen Jesus to humanity, bearing with him the forgiveness of our sins. Even in the face of the rejection of Jesus, the response of the Father of love is to love, to open up another way between human beings and himself and to do this in the gift of the Risen Lord, bearing with him the gift of the indwelling Spirit. And so with the risen Lord gathering his disciples together and giving them the gift of his Spirit, the initiative of God in Jesus the Christ continues in and around that group of disciples, the Church.

The understanding and practice of the sacrament of penance needs to be permeated and shaped by the mystery of the death and resurrection of Jesus. The contemporary formula of absolution expresses this well:

> God, the Father of mercies, through the death and resurrection of his Son, has reconciled the world to himself and has sent the Holy Spirit among us for the forgiveness of sins: through the ministry of the Church may God give you pardon and peace, and I absolve you from all your sins in the name of the Father, and of the Son and of the Holy Spirit.

The first part of the formula makes memory of the mystery of Christ's death and resurrection; the second part expresses and applies it sacramentally in the sacrament of penance.

Chapter 8

Conversion:
Living in Memory of Christ

The paschal mystery of Jesus' death and resurrection, which we considered in the previous chapter, is the reference point for, and the substance of, each sacrament and so of the sacrament of penance. Each sacrament is celebrated in memory of his death and resurrection in a way unique to that sacrament. It is celebrated in terms of the particular dimension or dimensions of human life to which that sacrament corresponds. The particular dimensions relevant to the sacrament of penance are those of sin, conversion and forgiveness but its even more specific concern is conversion. The sacrament of penance is the sacrament of conversion. In this chapter, we will again have recourse to the biblical reality of memorial to develop our understanding of conversion. We will start with a biblical view of the commandments.

Memorial and the commandments

Earlier on, when speaking of memorial, we touched briefly on the scriptural view of the Ten Commandments as gifts of God. They are the ten words of God given to his people as life-bearing gifts. Their observance is a means of access to the God of the Exodus. This locates the commandments within the memorial tradition of Israel. We need to see them as more than laws if we are to see their importance in the Old Testament and, for that matter, in the New.

The commandments are part of Israel's history with God. Israel is called to keep the commandments and to do so in memory of the Exodus (Exod 20:1-21; Deut 6:4-22; 7:17-26; 8:1-6; 9:7). Brevard Childs, in his *Memory and Tradition in*

Israel, expresses this understanding of the commandments in the following quotation:

> The commandments are not expressions of abstract law, but are events, a part of God's redemptive history toward Israel. Present Israel stands in an analogous situation with the people of Exodus. Israel is still being tested. The covenant history of Yahweh with his people continues ... Memory serves to link the present commandments as events with the covenant history of the past.[1]

Explaining this further, the commandments are sometimes seen as merely preserving, protecting and enforcing certain moral values by enunciating a series of prohibitions. By contrast, the above quotation from Childs makes it clear just how deeply the writer of the Deuteronomic tradition in the Bible sees the commandments as essentially tied into God's continuing action for his people, an action first revealed in the Exodus. The Deuteronomic tradition relates the commandments to the memory of the Exodus in such a way that the observance of the commandments is seen to provide for each generation of Israelites continuing access to the action of God in the Exodus. The action of God liberated his people from slavery; it extends now into the continuing life of the people through their obedience to the commandments.[2] Obeying the commandments is not just a matter of doing the right thing or of keeping a code whose purpose is social order and peace; it is rather to place oneself in the way of discovering the liberating God. Those things prohibited by the commandments are seen as having the capacity to enslave human beings. Each prohibition highlights for us not just bad social behaviour but something capable of enslaving us and so of being the equivalent of 'Pharoah' in Egypt. Dishonour to one's parents, murder and its violence, the lie, idols, the power of distorted desire and envy within us, the undiscerned use of our sexuality are seen as things capable of bringing about such enslavement. The Gospels, in their treatment of the commandments, highlight the powerful inner forces that the commandments seek to identify as capable of controlling human beings. We see this particularly in such passages as Matthew 5:20-48 in which the commandments are stripped back to the power for ill behind their prohibitions; so for instance, we find:

> 'You have heard that it was said to those of ancient times, "You shall not murder"; and "whoever murders shall be liable to judgment". But I say to you that if you are angry with a brother or sister, you will be liable to judgment; and if you insult a brother or sister, you will be liable to the council; and if you say, "You fool", you will be liable to the hell of fire. So when you are offering your gift at the altar, if you remember that your brother or sister has something against you, leave your gift there before the altar and go; first be reconciled to your brother or sister, and then come and offer your gift.' (Matt 5:21-24)

It is by keeping the commandments given by God that the people of Israel, and all human beings, are led into the way of freedom from slavery to these 'powers' among us and within us. For the biblical writers obedience to God's commandments (see Deut Chs 5-9) is a means of encountering in the present, in the face of different forms of slavery, the liberating God of the Exodus. The commandments, like all the words of God, are a 'light for our path', enlightening our blindness to the power of evil which is among us. We are easily tempted to confuse good and evil and so to give ourselves over to things which can reduce us to slavery. In the light of biblical revelation there are moral states and decisions which can hold us in their power as truly as Pharoah held the Israelites of old in his power. This understanding of God's commandments and his life-giving word is background to the importance of the accounts of the Temptations of Jesus in each of the Synoptic Gospels and of the temptations put in his way by the people among whom he lived, as we saw in the previous chapter.

Through the giving of the commandments, God continues to deliver his people from slavery. In obeying the commandments, or in disregarding them, the people are placing themselves in the way of freedom or of slavery, of life or of death (Deut 30:15-20). In obeying the commandments or in disregarding them Israel lives in memory of the Exodus or in forgetfulness of it; it continues on the path of freedom or of enslavement.

There is a great dilemma in all of this. Israel's experience, and ours, is that these 'powers' named and made the subject of prohibitions by the commandments are indeed 'powers' that hold us in their thrall. St Paul, in his writings, especially Romans and Galatians, discourses upon the law and its powerlessness to rescue us from these powers. The law shows us what is right but we find ourselves unable to obey it because those things from which it seeks to guard us have power in us. In his letter to the Romans, he says:

> For we know the law is spiritual; but I am of the flesh, sold into slavery under sin. I do not understand my own actions. For I do not do what I want, but I do the very thing I hate ... So I find it to be a law that when I want to do what is good, evil lies close at hand. For I delight in the law of God in my inmost self, but I see in my members another law at war with the law of my mind, making me captive to the law of sin that dwells in my members. Wretched man that I am! Who will rescue me from this body of death? Thanks be to God through Jesus Christ our Lord! (7:14-15, 21-25)

This passage of Paul points to the Good News proclaimed by Jesus and to the Gospels which proclaim him.

Jesus came proclaiming the kingdom of God, that is, the power of God, the ability of God to show his power among human beings. The Gospels show this power at work in Jesus' healing the sick, exorcising demons, calling disciples to himself, and forgiving sinners. In all this, God begins to reign, to show the workings of his power.

Jesus' actions with sinners, his sayings about sin and his parables open up a new way. That way tackles the problem in which Paul sees the law to be caught and which he sees the Lord resolving. Jesus comes to sinners, he mixes with them, and he scandalises those who see themselves as 'keeping the law' by this easy mixing with sinners. He is 'the hand God stretches out to sinners'.[3] In Jesus, God comes to the sinner; the sinner does not have to find the way to God. Jesus is himself the way and the truth and the life.

Jesus also unearths the power of sin in those who consider themselves sinless: we see this happening in the accounts of the adulterous woman (John 8:1-11), the Pharisee and the publican (Luke 18:9-14), the speck and the beam (Matt 7:1-5). Jesus not only does not exclude the sinner or even wait for them to come to him: he goes out after the stray and brings them back rejoicing (Luke 15). Jesus offers his company to the recognised sinners of his time, which scandalises those by whom they are condemned and who, subsequently, condemn him in their 'righteousness' (Mark 2:15-17; Matt 9:10-13; Luke 5:27-32).

As we saw in the previous chapter, the sin-infected attitudes and decisions of human beings brought about the death of Jesus. It involved the decisions of individuals, social and political movements, human cowardice, fear and distorted judgment. His death came about as a result of the power of those enslaving forces for which the commandments were given to bring into the light. Those powers were all there in the human beings acting in the lead-up to his death and in his death itself: violence and the murder it leads to, injustice, misuse of power, envy, fear, the contagious anger of the mob, the silence and fear of the little ones lost in forces greater than themselves.

In bringing Jesus to death, these forces were themselves ensnared in the non-violent love of God. In killing Jesus, they were themselves overcome by that power of God Jesus proclaimed and brought into the world. They were caught in love's trap. The Lord Jesus raised out of the death imposed on him is the manifestation of what the power of God does and will do among us.

Memorial and conversion

From what we have seen immediately above, there are two things that we are to live 'in memory of', regarding the sacrament of penance. The first is the liberating victory of God over sin in the death and resurrection of Jesus, and the second is Jesus' relationship to sinners and his words about them.

The first issues in the gift of forgiveness. It is given by the God who has shown himself and his attitude to sinful humanity in the death and resurrection of Jesus. Then in a second instance, this gift, since it is a gift which sets out to transform us, sets up a dialogue between us and the words of Jesus which leads us into conversion as a way of life. This is God's work in us to which we must open ourselves in order that it may happen (2 Cor 5:16-21).

This conversion is a continuing process for every Christian; in principle, it cannot be complete in the course of our biological lives because such life is itself an incomplete process, although it moves us forwards into our future. As human beings, our lives go through many phases and stages and each of them draws out something more of ourselves. To put this in the language we have been using, as we live out our lives we discover that we are 'living out of and living out' many different things from our past, some of which are positive and some negative. As the Christian lives, they find that among the things they are 'living out of and living out', there are those which are incompatible with 'living out of and living out' the memory of Jesus. This can happen at any of the many phases or stages of our lives and so we are always in need of conversion. We are always being called to convert to a further or deeper 'living in memory of Jesus'.

Conversion to 'living in memory of Jesus': (1) our human inheritance

To elaborate the meaning of conversion as living in memory of Jesus, I want to take up again the example used in the previous chapter of children living in memory of their parents. They do this within the long line of tradition or memory of which they and their parents are part. Children live in memory of their parents, that is, they live out of them and they live out what they have received from them – even if in reaction! Each person has to come to identify their place in this line of tradition, accept it and live it freely in their own unique way. This is the basic meaning of 'Honour your father and your mother'. It is the recognition of our place in the line of a tradition or in a 'life in memory'. This relationship is not of course the only strand of the highly complex human inheritance to which we interiorly belong but it is a core strand of it.

We all live in memory of our parents: we draw life from them not just physically but personally and spiritually and in terms of our social and cultural inheritance. At the same time, we live out their memory, that is, by being our parents, they set up dynamics in us by which what we have received from them continues to shape our attitudes, our feelings and our actions in the present. We live in an inner dialogue with them, being shaped by them yet transcending them as individual persons. This is the reality of memorial: to live out of something and to live it out; these two dimensions of our lives are as the two sides of a coin.

The pluses and minuses of this fundamental relationship with one's parents are present in every human being and each one of us lives out of them and lives them out without any necessarily explicit awareness of doing so. Thus, for example, when people experience marital problems, the problems can often be traced back to attitudes absorbed in their families of origin: such attitudes are in all of us because of the psychological, spiritual and cultural osmosis which has gone on between us and our parents and family. We live out of and live out many crucial early experiences of our life involving our immediate family and the society and culture of which we are part. As we live out our lives we find many inner dynamics at work in us which determine, or can at least very easily determine, our behaviour. Each human being could put forward examples of such inner dynamics of their personality from their own experience of life.

Further, through our parents and family, we live in a society and a culture which we live out of and live out in our individual and social lives. In and through our parents and immediate family we absorb a culture, a society's ingrained way of life, values and structures. Our parents and family are, in their own ways, images of the society in which they have their being. All these people interact creatively with a child in such a way that that child – in its own uniqueness – is made in their image and in the image of the society of which these people are themselves images.

Each person then, in their unique way lives out of and lives out this inheritance from family and culture, that is, lives in memory of it. This is both profoundly individually personal and profoundly rooted in the social group. This inheritance situates our freedom and provides a background whose value we have to discern in the process of taking possession of ourselves. We 'live out of and we live out' this inheritance as part of the human family.

Conversion to 'living in memory of Jesus': (2) the inheritance from Jesus

The memorial tradition of the Old and New Testaments works within this overall human dynamic of memorial. The word of God, and the communion established with God represented in the history of this tradition of revelation, has its own particular influence on the way human beings live memorially.

To understand this further we could again begin with the commandments. These, as we saw, are a way of encountering the freedom-giving God of the Exodus who, in these commandments, seeks to free human beings from the slavery named by these prohibitions.

A particular form of human 'living in memory' is established in the biblical tradition. The commandments, like virtually all else in Israel, were seen in the light of the Exodus. This was the experience of God under the leadership of Moses which gradually shed light on Israel's history and began to create new forms and ways of human life on the basis of this discovery of God, the One who desires to set human beings free. This same God led his people by means of leaders and prophets to keep seeing their life anew in his light. His word was a light for their path.

One dimension of this new understanding and living of human life given in the dialogue with the word of God is the discovery of the ambiguity of our human life, that is, that its goodness is spoiled by evil. Along with this, the origin of the presence of that evil is presented as mysterious and yet, at least in part, as attributable to negative human actions. This negative human action is described as sinful, as that which is contrary to the fundamental goodness of our humanity which has come to us in God's breathing his breath of life into us (Gen 2:7).

We live out of and live out this ambiguous nature of our humanity. The Bible is a unique book in that it is full of the stories of a people and of particular persons and it makes no attempt to avoid the profound ambiguity of the people whose book it is or of the various persons within that people whose stories it is particularly focused on telling. This ambiguity is clearly presented to us in the historical books of the Bible, in the writings of the prophets, in the Wisdom literature and in the foundational story of the Exodus presented in the first five books of the Bible. It is presented in a particularly concentrated and symbolic form in the story of the creation and fall and the accompanying narratives of the first eleven chapters of the book of Genesis. Goodness distorted by the presence of evil is beautifully portrayed in the figures of the story of the creation and the fall, of Cain and Abel, and of the Tower of Babel.

In these highly figurative narratives, symbols are offered to us as mirrors into which each generation may look to see something of the inner dynamics of its own humanity: light is shed on it by continuing the dialogue with the word of God which occurred in the biblical tradition. To interpret these stories as historical is to miss the point of their importance and relevance; they are there to show us our own humanity in our own present moment. All these scriptural writings are a light on the inheritance out of which we live as human beings and they form in the people who make them their own a particular memory influenced by the biblical revelation of God.

As the biblical tradition continues into the New Testament, the death and resurrection of Jesus reshapes our understanding of human life by giving it a future: the future of the resurrection. Thus we are invited to live as if there were no death! It invites us to live out of and live out that death and resurrection as the radical discovery of the meaning and value of human life. It invites us to live as Jesus lived! This involves us in a conversion, a change of mind, a change of point of view on life. This is the work of God in us and it is the work of a lifetime.

The sayings, actions and parables of Jesus are much more powerful and far-reaching than moral instruction. In fact we find in the Gospels little direct moral instruction. Jesus' words and actions unearth things in us, yet often puzzle us. So much is this so that people often put his words aside as too idealistic or other-worldly. I would like to suggest that we need to see his words, such as those making up the Sermon on the Mount, in the light of memorial, as we have been speaking about it. His words often act to discomfort us or dislodge our presumptions of what is right and wrong or to disturb our facile reduction of God's word to our values.

In hearing his words, we are hearing words which seek to create a displacement within us. 'Blessed are the poor in spirit; theirs is the kingdom of Heaven' is what St Paul would describe as a two-edged sword cutting between bone and marrow. It questions a basic human assumption that it is good to be rich and that riches are a blessing from God; it raises questions and stirs up our presumptions. The words of Jesus question 'what we live out of and what we live out'; they question us on what 'we live in memory of' and they call us to live in memory of the God whom Jesus proclaims, the one who raises the dead to life. The words of Jesus create an interaction with our memory in order to bring us to new life 'in memory of him'.

His words also unearth the sinful dimension of human life. The parables about sin and forgiveness and the stories about his mixing with sinners often turn the tables on those who see themselves as sinless. He is ever inviting people to see in those they regard as sinners, the sin that is also in themselves. This is clear in the parable of the Prodigal Son, the Pharisee and the publican, the incident with the adulterous woman and the saying about the speck or the beam in the eye. We need to let his words reshape our minds to discover what God sees as truly sinful.

In Jesus' call to us to change the ways we see things (Mark 1:15), in the unsettling effect which his words have upon us, in his rejection of his disciples' attitudes, in his refusals to go along with the ways of the people or of their leaders, we see him at work seeking to suggest change to the ways of human beings. In this he is inviting us into a new way of living, into a new 'living in memory'. In his overcoming the destructive power of human sinfulness exercised against himself in his death, we discover our deliverance from the power of human destructiveness.

The following of Jesus issues us into a new form of life – a life in memory of him, that is, of his discovery and revelation of God, a life shaped by the memory of his attitudes and actions. This living in memory of Jesus asks the Christian to be changed, to repent, to allow the influence of Jesus and his Spirit to draw them away from those elements of human inheritance which his word shows up as sinful. This involves conversion which is not just a different way of acting but a different way of thinking, a different way of seeing things; it seeks to change our presence and action in the world. This conversion is not achieved in a single decision or moment but involves a long-term shift in our way of life: a shift from human life lived without Christ's light to human life lived in his light, a light which gradually reveals the shadows within us and unearths the dynamics at work in our humanity for good or for ill.

Conversion

Christian conversion is a lifelong task, and it is the work of God in us. Conversion is like migration. A person migrating from one society and culture to another enters into a long process of change which involves their individual and social identity. It goes through many stages. So it is with the process of conversion. Migrants leave their own culture and move into another. They begin by feeling strangers in the new culture: everything around them is different – the food, the language, the way people think and act, the system of government. In turn, all these things fall back on quite subtle perceptions of reality which are present in every culture and which are different in different cultures.

As time goes on, new migrants living in that different culture and participating in its ways of doing things reap benefits from the new situation and become accustomed to it. There are in-between times when they live publicly as if they belonged to the new culture and domestically as if they belonged to their culture of origin. Their use of the language of the new culture symbolises their situation: it will bear the sounds native to their culture of origin filtering through the phrases and forms of the new language.

This process can be described in terms of 'memory': of living out these two cultures and of living out of them.

Migrants are in an in-between state in which both cultures are having their effect on them. Along the way such persons will have to make choices which will shift their alignment towards one culture or the other.

Just as the migrant lives in an in-between situation, living out of and living out two cultural realities, so the Christian lives in a parallel situation. In the Christian case this is called 'conversion'. Like the change going on in the migrant, the change in the person seeking to live out of and live out the memory of Jesus is a lifelong process and it forms them as a whole. It is a process which is not just about making a decision to follow Christ but one which needs to penetrate our whole selves and which takes a lifetime. It involves each person in the many phases and stages of the process of conversion. As people live their lives in dialogue and interplay with the word of God, light is thrown on the journey into which they are called and this light leads them to live in Christ's memory.

The sacrament of penance

Looking at conversion in terms of memorial, as we have done in this chapter, involves a re-conceiving and a reshaping of the sacrament of penance which is the sacrament of conversion. The very word 'conversion' has a different background and 'flavour' from words such as 'repentance' and 'penance', both of which have similar root meanings to 'conversion' but whose histories have associated them with different mentalities and practices which have left them with a different 'flavour' to their meaning.

Looking at the sacrament of penance as the sacrament of conversion and seeing conversion and the moral life in terms of memorial necessarily shifts us away from other forms of conceiving the sacrament, particularly one that looks at it in more legal and juridical imagery.

In dealing with the history of the sacrament of penance, we have seen that there have been several models at work in the various penitential institutions of the Church. This remains a very important insight. One of the current problems we have with this sacrament is the rather juridical imagery that has been predominantly, but not exclusively, associated with it in the recent past. This imagery involved conceiving the sacrament as a tribunal, conceiving one's sins as offences against a law, using the Ten Commandments in a legal and casuistic way as the means of examining one's conscience, and conceiving forgiveness rather like acquittal by a judge. This imagery is one that has been used widely in the history of the tradition.

A particular emphasis on the juridical image for this sacrament began in the period when absolutism was beginning to come to dominance, from the fourteenth century on. The cultural and political mood of the time carried through into the religious dimension of the culture. We dealt with this shift in understanding which put the emphasis on God's will when dealing with the theologian, Duns Scotus, in Chapter Five. From that period on, absolution – as God's act administered by the priest – was increasingly seen as the essence of the sacrament and the acts of the penitent (contrition, conversion and satisfaction) were downplayed; yet St Thomas Aquinas would have given equal weight to each of them as part of the essence of the sacrament. The cultural influences on this imagery for the sacrament enable us to relativise such imagery and set us seeking imagery more suited to our sensibilities and religious needs and, indeed, to the gospel origins of the sacrament.

Even though many theologians would have continued to maintain the position of St Thomas, practice tended to take on the view that absolution was what mattered. This may have been because it was the easiest way pastorally: since people had difficulty in giving expression to their sins in their confession and there were questions about the depth and quality of their contrition, to see absolution alone as the essence of the sacrament made the whole process practically and pastorally workable. Since this view fitted the mood of the time and worked pastorally, its spread was irresistible.

This practice, however, made the role of the penitent secondary. What they had to confess and their attitudes were necessary prerequisites to the giving of absolution but not essential parts of the sacrament. So they tended to be neglected. The sacrament of penance became the sacrament of forgiveness! The conversion of the penitent, which was what was being sacramentalised in the sacrament, tended to become quite secondary. Instead of the sacrament being seen as the sacramentalisation of conversion (penance), it was conceived as the ritual in which God forgave us our sins.

We began this chapter looking at the sacraments from a point of view suggested by the biblical tradition – that of memorial. This is deeply rooted not only in the Bible but in our continuing tradition, particularly as that involves the sacraments. I would suggest that what we have seen above about 'living in memory of Jesus' offers us much more fertile ground in which to look at the sacrament of penance or of conversion. This can give new life to our understanding of conversion and its sacrament.

Notes

1. Brevard Childs, *Memory and Tradition in Israel* (London: SCM Press Ltd, 1962) 51.

2. ibid., 50-6. Given the importance of the concept of 'memorial' in what follows, I would refer readers, in addition to the work of Brevard Childs, to the following works: Joseph Blenkinsopp, 'Memory, Tradition and the Construction of the Past in Ancient Israel', *Biblical Theology Bulletin* (1997, n. 3) 76-82; George Lacey, 'Eucharist as the Intersection between Memory and Forgetfulness', *Worship* (2003, n. 1) 52-6; Bruce T. Morrill, *Anamnesis as Dangerous Memory* (Collegeville, MN: The Liturgical Press, 2000); Max Thurian, *The Eucharistic Memorial*, Vols 1 and 2 (London:

Lutterworth Press, 1960, 1961); Claus Westermann, 'The Representation of History in the Psalms', in *Praise and Lament in the Psalms* (Altanta: John Knox Press, 1981) 2214-45.

3. cf. *Eucharistic Prayer for Masses of Reconciliation II.*

Chapter 9

Sin: A Human Reality, a Biblical Discovery

One of the things most spoken about when discussing the crisis of the sacrament of penance today is the loss of the sense of sin. There certainly has been a change in the way people in our culture, including many Christians, think about sin. Many ways of behaving that would have been considered seriously sinful in the recent past would not now be seen as such by many people; this especially applies in the area of sexuality. In this chapter we will look further into what we mean by 'sin'. This I believe is a huge topic beyond anything I am able to deal with thoroughly so I merely wish to suggest what I see as some useful perspectives towards a deeper understanding of sin in our time.

To state the obvious: the biblical revelation involves a particular discovery of the human reality which we recognise as part of our life and the life of all human beings, that is, our sinfulness. The sacrament of penance is a Christian way of dealing with it.

The sacraments of initiation – baptism, confirmation and Eucharist – establish us as Christians. In each of the other sacraments, dimensions of human life within the community of faith find ecclesial expression. Thus in the other four sacraments, Christian expression is given to the significant dimensions of: illness and its shadow, death (anointing of the sick), sinfulness (penance), relationship (marriage), and human social structuring, involving such things as leadership, authority, power and service (orders).

In the sacrament of penance, we are dealing with the Christian discovery of, and particular slant on, the sinfulness which is part of all humanity. That human evil which we do to each other or suffer at each other's hands is seen in relation to God as revealed by Christ. This sinfulness is not just a matter of actions but of a state of sinfulness which is expressed in action. It reveals a deep wound in our humanity so often expressed in the dividedness and lack of harmony in and between human societies and individuals and indeed within the individual person. This in turn finds expression in violence in its many forms. Human history teaches us that this human evil cannot easily be removed as it keeps recurring in various forms, generation after generation.

In the sacrament of penance we are dealing with that same reality of sin in the Christian community and in individual Christians. It is the 'sinfulness' common to all human beings which is lived in the Church in explicit dialogue with the revealing word of Christ and with his death and resurrection. It is in this dialogue with God's word that we discover sin specifically to be that which is in opposition to God's way as revealed in Christ.

The sinfulness which we deal with in the sacrament of penance is humanity's sinfulness. It is part of the woof and weave of that humanity of which we are part and, in dealing with that sinfulness 'in memory of Jesus', we deal not just with our own sinfulness but with that which is in all human beings. We deal with it in ourselves who make up the Church and in the Church as a human group made up of all that makes up humanity.

This finds a parallel in the sacrament of the anointing of the sick. The illness which is 'celebrated' in the sacrament is not a specifically Christian phenomenon. It is the illness to which all humankind is subject. It is 'celebrated' in the sacrament in a specifically Christian way.

In these two sacraments, we are dealing with sin and illness, which we claim have been overcome in Christ's death and resurrection. We claim that he has overcome the power of sin to separate us from God and to damage the harmony and life God gives, just as we claim that he has overcome the power of death of which illness is the sign. We claim that Christ's resurrection out of death has freed us from the destructive power of these two things yet they continue to violate our human world. They seem to laugh in the face of our claim of Christ's victory over them.

However, just as Jesus died and was raised out of death without an obvious overturning of the world's state, so do these sacraments work in that same quiet way. The victory which Christ enables over illness and death, which it brings in its train (either immediately or remotely), is shown in the presence of gifts of the Risen Lord in the ill person, namely peace and serenity in the face of diminishment and death. These gifts of the Holy Spirit of the risen One in the ill person are the sign and seed of Christ's already-present victory over death. In that peace and serenity, death is already overcome.

So with the sacrament of penance, sin does not disappear from the life of the penitent or of the Church; it is a permanent thread in the woof and weave of our human condition. But the forgiven sinner knows that the power of sin is no longer able to enslave and consume him or her even though it is still present in their lives; the Church knows that the sin that can be even scandalisingly present in its life will not win out over the power of Christ whose Spirit always continues to give life. The power of sin has been robbed of its capacity to make us its own. There is a power greater than it which can loosen the bonds in which it would keep us shackled.

This is not only about the individual sinner or even the community of faith alone. This is about all of humankind of which the Church is the sacrament. The sacrament of penance in its very liturgical unfolding manifests the Church which is the sacrament of humankind. It is the sacrament, or sign and instrument, of that ultimate unifying and healing which God is at work everywhere seeking to bring about.

Seeing the sacrament in this way is seeing it in terms of the concept of the Church put forward in the documents of the Second Vatican Council. The core activities of the Church, the sacraments, are activities of that group of people chosen from the midst of humankind to be the sign and instrument or sacrament of what God the lover of humankind seeks to do in humanity's midst.

This has important practical consequences for the celebration of the sacrament of penance. We need to see the sinfulness with which we are concerned in the sacramental or in non-sacramental forms of penance as manifesting the real sinfulness that we see in our world around us. The celebration of penance – sacramental or non-sacramental – is not concerned with an inwardly turned sense of sin, which can seem trivial in the light of the evil we see at work in our world, but with identifying and acknowledging that same sin as it appears in us. This is in order to bring that sin into the light of Christ's words, to acknowledge it as ours, to bring it before the healing power of God and to encourage our 'living in memory of Christ'. This also places us, as the Church, in our right relationship to humankind.

Sinner: scapegoat or symbol?

One of the constant perspectives offered by the Gospels on sin and the sinner is that of seeing the sinner as symbol rather than as scapegoat. Human history is full of examples of pinpointing others and scapegoating them as the source of evil and then of excluding them in some way from the community. Their exclusion pretends to rid the community of evil; their exclusion also involves violence.

In this scapegoating the sinner is identified as the bearer of sin and the separation of the sinner from the surrounding community or social group is seen as the means of excluding sin from the group. In expulsion or exclusion rituals, this is the case. A person, or persons, or a particular group is identified as the sinner or the cause of social disharmony or the reason for the anger of the gods, and those so identified are then excluded from the group in order to save the group from the threat of break-up or from dangers consequent upon the displeasure of the gods.

In this situation, there is a presumption that the 'sinner', individual or group, is the exclusive bearer of evil and that their exclusion will leave the group clean or pure or out of danger. This attribution of all evil to the scapegoat leaves the group blind to its own continuing evil and prepares the ground for further destructive threats to the community from the hidden source of evil or disruption to which their own scapegoating action has blinded them. This promotes violence against those scapegoated and self-righteousness in those who do the excluding. The anthropologist and literary critic cum theologian, René Girard, whose works are having considerable influence, has developed the understanding of this scapegoating mechanism along a particular line. He sees it as an integral part of the whole process of human redemption which culminates in Jesus. He sees it as an essential thread of the development of the biblical revelation which culminates in the scapegoating of Jesus and in Jesus' bringing to the surface this hidden, powerful mechanism which has always produced and continues to produce a false sense of salvation among human beings who, in scapegoating, are deepening their blindness to their real situation.[1]

We find several incidents in the Gospels where Jesus speaks to this situation and they are crucial to a gospel understanding of sin and forgiveness and so of the sacrament of penance. A strong presentation of this perspective is in John 8:1-11, the story of the adulterous woman. The woman is dragged before Jesus, having been caught in the very act of committing adultery. The opponents of Jesus say that the law demands that she be stoned to death and they ask him what he has to say. His final response, 'Let the one without sin cast the first stone', makes precisely the point at issue here. Formulating it in the terms suggested above, we could ask: Is this woman seen as the sole sinner while her accusers are free of sin and so is she a scapegoat? Or: Is she a bearer of the sinfulness that is in them all, and so is she a symbol of the sinfulness that is in all? Is she the only one with sin, so that dealing with her deals with the whole issue of sin, leaving everyone else sinless and pure? Or: Is she a symbol, that is, is there in her what is in everyone else present at that scene? If the latter is the case, then she is a mirror into which everyone can look to see what is in themselves. This is clearly Jesus' understanding.

There is a similar situation at work in the parable of the Pharisee and the publican (Luke 18:9-14). The Pharisee at the front of the Temple presents himself before God as 'all good' and quite unlike 'this publican here' who, in the Pharisee's mind, is a sinner. Yet it is the publican, sinner indeed, who, having said 'Lord, be merciful to me a sinner', goes home at rights with God. The Pharisee makes the clear separation of himself from the sinner, scapegoating the publican by his own self-righteousness.

The statement of Jesus in the Sermon on the Mount that we should take the plank out of our own eye before taking the speck out of our brother's or sister's eye (Matt 7:1-5) makes the same point.

This scapegoating, the identification of the other alone as sinner, is based on a blindness which is the source of so much evil in our human world. It is utterly crucial that we come to see in the sinner, one who is like ourselves, one who acts as a mirror reflecting back to us the sinfulness that is within each of us. It is so often blindness or the incapacity to hear which is presented as the real source of sinfulness in the Gospels. When we reflect on the evil that is part of our human history, of the history of the Church, and of our own individual history, it is so often blindness which has led to the ongoing evils which prove so difficult to heal.

The question of the sinner as symbol or scapegoat is important for the understanding and celebration of the sacrament of penance. We can see from the earliest form of the sacrament, which did indeed have an exclusion structure, that the question of the sinner as symbol or scapegoat was implicitly present. It is also clear that the Church saw the sinner as symbol.

In that first historical form of penance, the penitents were not totally excluded from the community. They became – like the catechumens – a particular group within the overall community. They remained a part of the overall household of the faith without being able to come to its heart, which consists in participation at the eucharistic table. They were not expelled but were differently included in the life of the community. This indicates an attitude which sees them on the same journey as other Christians but as having to make that journey in a more severe way because of their fall into very serious sin. So they were treated as symbols of the conversion going on in the whole community.

The rigorist reaction to the reconciliation of penitents in the early Church also witnesses to the fact that sinners were not separated totally from it, as the rigorists desired. The mainstream Church did not see the Church as a pure community set apart from sinners but as a community of penitents, all of whose members were in some way continuing to do penance. This is witnessed to by their emphasis on penance for daily sins as well. The rigorists, on the other hand, saw the reconciliation of penitents as an abuse, precisely because their attitude to the sinners was one of scapegoating.

In a detailed study of the Rite of Reconciliation of Penitents in Rome in the fifth and sixth centuries, François Bussini looks at the meaning of the liturgical words and actions used in the rite. One of the points he makes is about the relationship of the *circumstantes* (those standing around) to the penitents, that is, the relationship of the assembled community of the Church to the penitents being reconciled. This relationship is shown in the liturgical actions of the *circumstantes*: the *circumstantes*, as the word suggests, are standing while the penitents are *jacentes*, that is, prostrate. And yet both groups are weeping and, in this, those standing express their identification with the prostrate penitents. In this instance, the rest of the community participates in the journey of the penitents to reconciliation. They are brothers and sisters on the same journey, subject to the same frailty, and members of the one and same body of Christ. The liturgical actions of the assembly show both communion with, and difference from, the penitents.[2]

We can also see in later practices of penance the continuing recognition on the part of the bishop or the priest-confessor that they also were sinners. We find this presumed in the case of the bishop in the Romano-Germanic Pontifical of the tenth century in which the bishop recognises himself as a sinner before acting as confessor.[3] And we find it for priest-confessors in the earliest emerging forms of private penance.[4]

Lent became a penitential season for the whole Church from the tenth century on and this practice in itself showed a unity between penitents and all the other members of the Church as these latter began to participate in rites which were originally specifically for the public penitents only.

The sinner is symbol. In the person in whom sin is recognised we are not dealing with something foreign to us as Christians or as human beings but with something which is part of the human condition which we all share. This is one of the foundations of the ecclesial dimension of the sacrament of penance – a dimension of the sacrament which needs clear expression for its effective celebration.

Seeing the sinner as symbol is also important in the process of discerning sin in ourselves. As we look towards those people or situations which are clearly identified as sinful in our society, we have mirrors in which to look to discover either our own sinfulness, or the scapegoating mechanisms of our own society.

Acknowledging our sin

Speaking about the sinner as symbol or scapegoat provides an excellent context in which to look at the importance of the acknowledgment of sin. The recognition and acknowledgment of sin is an aspect of the repentance for which the gospel calls. Such acknowledgment has taken place in several forms in the history of the Church.

In acknowledging our sin, we ground that sin in ourselves as its perpetrator; the guilt and blame involved in it are thereby tied in with their proper origin and the influence of the sin is contained. In such acknowledgment the sin is owned and its provenance is known.

Is there not a tendency within us to avoid such acknowledgment or confession? This urge may be tied in with a deep and barely named fear that, if we are known to be sinners, we will be cast aside and excluded from human society, that our standing will be destroyed and perhaps we ourselves with it. This fear finds expression in the Genesis myth of the Fall which presents Adam and Eve as not being able to be themselves with each other or with God. They hide because they are naked (Gen 3:8-13). Then, significantly, they scapegoat each other rather than acknowledge their sin: 'it was the woman you put with me who made me eat it', says Adam; 'it was the snake', says Eve (Gen 3:12-13). There is even an attempt to blame God in Adam's statement that it was the woman God put with him who was the cause of the problem. In the narrative their sin results in their being excluded from the place where they ought to be, according to their Creator's plan: the Garden of Paradise, where all is harmony.

We can discern this human fear of acknowledging our sin in the scapegoating process which is so prominent a part of our human history and which has deep roots in our human psyche and culture.[5] Exclusion is not only a societal, juridical and religious process but it is embedded in our everyday living and attitudes, in the course of which we can, by words and actions, exclude people from our company, exclude them from among those who properly belong and even exclude them from among those who are properly human. The subtle interconnections of our belonging within a group make us very sensitive to the mores of the group and to the pressure subtly exerted to belong to it. Such pressure can be strong enough to create a blind acquiescence and a moral paralysis in people. It can force the exclusion of different or unwanted others. This can happen to people of different races, different religions, different sexual orientations, different opinions, or, in fact, to people bearing any kind of difference perceived as threatening. Such exclusion, or the threat of it, can be at work on the large political and social scale or it can be at work in the 'play' of children in school grounds. It is at work in subtle and everyday ways wherever there are human beings. This threat of exclusion as a power within our human world and our human psyches is an important root of our reluctance to acknowledge ourselves as sinners.

To acknowledge that the sinful acts which we have done are indeed ours is to rob them of much of their power to do evil. When we acknowledge them as ours, it becomes clear that they originate in us and not in someone else, whereas unacknowledged evil actions and words hang around in the atmosphere unclaimed and create mistrust and suspicion among those around us. When no one knows who did this or that or who said this or that, a process begins in which people more or less explicitly wonder if it was X or Y or Z who did or said it. It creates an atmosphere of suspicion. It opens the door to the prejudices already there, to the grudges, mistrusts and suspicions which are already a part of the social atmosphere. Such corruption of the social atmosphere occurs within families, among friends, in workplaces, in business, between ethnic groups and national communities and within the community of the Church.

The lack of acknowledgment of sin – the refusal to accept our part of the responsibility for doing ill – separates, divides and creates conflict and it infects further the already damaged human condition in which we live. Recognition and acknowledgment is already an act of reconciliation. It begins to clarify and purify the situation in which we live. It sheets home responsibility where it belongs and stops the false attribution of blame, the contamination of suspicion and the furtherance of scapegoating.

The importance of this acknowledgment applies in matters small and large. Its great importance is in the fact that we all live within a context which affects us intrinsically – we imbibe it from our earliest days. We in turn are responsible for the quality of the social atmosphere in which we live. We need to distinguish between individual responsibility and collective responsibility but we cannot separate them. Sin is never a purely individual matter: it always has a social, communal dimension to it.

To return to the beginning point of this section, even in small matters there is a form of scapegoating at work when we refuse to acknowledge our sin. Our refusal to recognise it has the potential to allow it to be attributed to others, to allow our shadow to fall on others. It is an implicit statement that we are sinless while others are sinners. It puts us in the position of those who accused the adulterous woman or in the position of the Pharisee in the parable of the Pharisee and the publican. It pretends there is no speck, or plank, in our own eye.

The discernment of sin: (1) historical considerations

The Church's perception of sin is influenced by its historical and cultural situation. Sin and its perception are not purely unchanging or abstract matters but occur within particular historical situations and are shaped in part by the circumstances of each historical period. Thus in each age the Church reads the Scriptures and lives its tradition within, and in dialogue with, the mentality of its time. There is a specific dialogue with the word of God set up within that mentality. We cannot withdraw from the mentality of our time or from the historical setting in which we live; we can, however, become critically aware of them. The Scriptures are not only read within a particular historical mentality but 'they read' that mentality and so provide a critique of it. That is, the Scriptures interact with that mentality and its age and shed their light on it. They bring the light of Christ to that situation and so form the ongoing tradition.

This basic historical character of our Christian tradition means that the perception of sin itself has a history. Each age will have specific perceptions of sin which reflect the sensitivities of that age. This brings changing emphases and new insights within the continuing tradition.

As far as I am aware, the history of the understanding of sin has not as yet been comprehensively studied. I would like to propose some reflections on it which may stimulate us to consider our current cultural difficulties in identifying sin, which is one of the problems generally recognised in regard to the sacrament of penance.[6]

Without any pretensions to an exhaustive treatment, I would propose that we can see four somewhat different conceptions of sin holding sway in four periods of the Church's life. Four cameos emerge from the long history of the Church's tradition in this area. I am suggesting that these conceptions flavour the sense of sin in their own age, even though they do not describe it comprehensively.

In the canonical penance of the first centuries of the Church's life, there were three major sins for which canonical penance was applied: *idolatry, murder* and *adultery.* These sins were regarded as making continuing membership of the community impossible for the perpetrator as they were seen to contradict the very nature of the community. In those centuries idolatry was a particularly clear example of a sin which contradicted the meaning of being a member of the Church. These three 'classic' sins were treated as sins against the community and, for perpetrators to return to the community, they had to repeat the process by which people became members of the community – as if that original process of initiation had been vitiated by such sins. The conception of serious sin at work here is intricately tied into the nature of the Church as a community with its own strong sense of identity set in a world which did not accept it and, at times, made a scapegoat of it. The historical situation of the Church was built into the way it conceived its paradigmatic 'sins'. These sins helped reveal the nature of the Church by being a negative image of it.[7]

The second instance I would suggest is the coming of St Columban to the continent of Europe in the 590s and, with him, his Penitential. In Columban's work, we have a good example of a refinement brought about by the gospel of a previous conception of wrong or sin. In the mentality of this period, sin was seen as a taboo, as an external offence against an injunction, object or person. That offence was particularly heinous when it was an offence against a sacred object, shrine or ritual. This sense of the 'taboo', of the committing of an offence even without regard for one's intention to do it or not, had been, and was to be, present in the minds of ordinary people for many centuries. Columban's Penitential, however, brought the gospel to bear on this presumed concept of sin and did this by a greater interiorisation of the sense of sin. He emphasised *internal sin* such as sins of desire which were considered sinful, even if the acts which could flow from them did not eventuate.

This brought an aspect of the Sermon on the Mount into play. In this way a conception of sin which was dominant in a barely Christianised society underwent some degree of conversion through the influence of the gospel.[8]

In a third instance, historians suggest that the paradigmatic sin of the Middle Ages could be seen as hatred or *social hostility*. Such behaviour constituted a threat to the unity of society which was of course a Christian society. This explains the horror in which heresy was held as the sin which most threatened the unity of the Christian society of the Middle Ages. This is also to be understood against the background of the long and hard struggle to achieve that unity which was so easily endangered by the vengefulness and ambitious violence of so many of the medieval magnates. Their culture was one of shame and honour in which offence led them into retaliation and feud. John Bossy, an historian of the later Middle Ages, suggests that such sins of hatred, vengeance and petty feuding in communities of all kinds was the paradigmatic sin of that time. He also suggests that, in this mindset, adultery was seen not only in the later, more directly sexual sense but also as an offence likely to badly disrupt the community in which the offenders lived, that is, as a sin against the unity of that community.[9]

Authors dealing with the decree of Lateran IV – that every Catholic should confess all their sins each year at Easter – note that the most common reason for the refusal of absolution (and so for non-reception of Communion at Easter, which was a very communal act) was offence against the peace of the community, such as the refusal to make peace with a neighbour.[10] The conception of sin in this period, therefore, was shaped by the fear of 'social hostility' and the Church sought to provide the needed antidote to it.

The fourth historical instance I would propose for reflection is one that began in the seventeenth century and continued into the twentieth. In this period, *sexual sin* provided the major cultural paradigm for the conception of sin. In this period a new sense of privacy came to prevail, one in which sexual behaviour was conceived as a private matter in a way that it had not previously been conceived. This was especially the case in the dominant and growing middle class. Gradually, as this period unfolded, an increasing division arose between public life and private life and a new importance was given to the immediate family as the place where one lived the more intimate side of life. Sexual behaviour became a matter which, in principle, belonged to this private sphere of life and came to be seen more and more as a matter for the married couple alone. It was part of their private life. The understanding of marriage also developed as a more private matter concerning the couple themselves rather than as a matter of family politics and economics.[11]

This transition was expressed in the way in which houses were built. In the place of the much more open living quarters (including sleeping quarters), which was characteristic of the Middle Ages, there arose the 'sexually built' house in which there was a bedroom for the parents, a bedroom for the boys and a bedroom for the girls. In the earlier situation, sexual activity could easily take place with others present; in the latter, it took place in the private area of the couple. This change in sexual culture symbolised a much broader shift in cultural sensibilities; it indicated and carried a new mentality.

In this situation and mentality, sexuality became a hidden, even secret, dimension of human lives. It is possible that this hiddeness played into the powerful presence of the sexual in human beings to give it a more tantalising power in human consciousness than it had previously had. It is in this context that we can find some explanation for the powerful influence of sexual sin as the paradigm of sin for the centuries between the seventeenth and twentieth centuries.

The wisdom writers in the Old Testament at times say that they have two things to say and yet a third. Here I would like to say that I have made four suggestions and now yet a fifth. In the post-Reformation period, there arose in the Catholic Church, a model of sin which revealed one's Catholic *identity*. Within the dominating Catholic-Protestant conflict of that time, such things as not going to Mass on Sunday, eating meat on Friday or marrying outside the Church became very serious sins and formed a very important type of sin. Each of these was tied into one's identity as a Catholic in a way not unlike the sins of idolatry, murder and adultery in the early Church. They certainly required confession before going to Communion and sometimes missing Mass was confessed even when it was quite impossible for the person involved to go to Mass. Given the changed situation since that post-Reformation period, these 'sins' are no longer thought of with the same seriousness. It is also interesting from the point of view of the historical shaping of our understanding of sin that such sins were seen as much more serious in countries where Catholics were a minority alongside a Protestant majority.

The above reflections and suggestions on some historical conceptions of sin have been presented on a very broad canvas and each conception can be seen not only as a tendency within the socio-religious awareness of those times but also as a tendency which gives us insight into the mind of the times. The point to be made from the above examples is that, in dealing with the discernment of sin, we believe and think within the historical situation and culture to which we belong. Our sense of sin has not come about outside our history and culture. We need to be aware of this as we look into such questions as the loss of a sense of sin in our age or, to put it more positively, the question of how we speak of an authentic sense of sin in our day. Historical perceptions of sin may be in tune or out of tune with the gospel; they may be more or less worthy of the Christian tradition: this is a matter to be discerned. What is crucial theologically is that we be aware of these cultural influences on our tradition, and of the genuine diversity of the conceptions of sin within our tradition. All such conceptions need to be seen within the context of the culture in which they arose, just as the conceptions of our own time need to be seen within the context of our time. The Christian character of these conceptions depends upon the interaction that occurs between them and the words and actions of Jesus in the Gospels as we have spoken about them earlier in this book. The history of moral theology is a clear illustration of the working out of the inherited tradition in dialogue with the culture and thought of various times. We can see this in the tradition's use of Platonism and Stoicism in patristic times and of Aristotelianism in the Middle Ages.[12]

In our discernment of sin today we need to be aware of the influences of the past on our sense of sin, for example, in regard to our view on sexual behaviour. We need to be aware of the new situation in which we are living and its influence on us, and of our absolutely necessary dialogue with the gospel without which there cannot be a Christian morality or a proper use of the sacrament of penance.

The discernment of sin: (2) contemporary considerations

We now begin to look at a question mentioned several times already, which is critical for the sacrament of penance: the discernment of sin. The sense of sin common among Catholic people a few decades ago seems to have changed; some would say that it has disappeared altogether. This is a huge question and one that we will only touch on in this book. It requires much more work to be done by pastors, theologians and experts in such sciences as psychology. It also requires careful listening to the voice of the faithful.

To outline this question, I would like to refer to the work of Anton Vergote, a theologian and psychologist, who deals explicitly with this changed sense of sin in our day. Vergote suggests that a shift has occurred over the last couple of centuries in people's sense of sin. The causes of this shift are hard to pinpoint because we are dealing with deep changes in human awareness over a long period of time. He suggests that the cultural and psychological underpinning of the sense of sin and the practice of the sacrament of penance which had prevailed among Catholics up to recent centuries have been undermined in this cultural shift and so do not function effectively any longer. In this he sees an example of the historical shaping of the sense of sin which we spoke about in the immediately preceding section of this chapter.[13]

He describes what he sees happening in the following way. The natural religiosity which gave people a sense of duty before God, and which was so important in earlier forms of Christianity – as well as in other religions – has disappeared and been replaced, both in the Christian community and in the Western world, with a sense of duty towards others. Along with this, and as part of it, an individual sense of morality particularly sensitive to sexual matters has given way to a more collective moral sense of social obligation.

Moreover, the psychological sciences have grown and become part of the presumed mentality of our culture. This has created a cultural attitude which believes that recourse to human technical means for remedying faults, seen as psychological wounds, is the effective way of dealing with them. There follows from this a questioning of the relevance of the confession of sins to have them forgiven.

The common cultural conviction that Christian morality is nothing other than a human morality which has been formed by 'many centuries' of civilisation, philosophical thought and Christian influence has taken over the foreground in the understanding of morality. This has replaced an understanding of morality as being about obedience to the law of God. In this recent situation, Christians see themselves as needing to be obedient to their own conscience rather than to authority and so the Church's authority has come into question, along with that of the priest in the sacrament of penance.[14]

All of this, in Vergote's opinion, brings up the absolute necessity for contemporary believers to have a much more deeply interiorised faith. The Christian tradition cannot have any bearing on, or moral authority in, a person's life unless it has begun to be integrated into a person's existence as an inner wellspring of their human and Christian existence. The use of the sacrament of penance depends upon this.

The above perspectives offered by Vergote raise questions rather than provide answers but they are questions which cannot be avoided. They are questions for which we do not as yet have satisfactory answers. We are in the midst of a process of working towards new perspectives arising from such questions. This book is written in the hope of providing some stimulus for that process.

Vergote's description of the contemporary situation (one of many possible descriptions) leads me back to what has so often been stated above: that it is the dialogue, the interplay between our human situation and the word of God which is crucial in this matter, as in so many others. In this interaction, the word of God is released to speak again and anew in our tradition. The Word Incarnate can speak again now in our circumstances as he spoke during his earthly life from within the circumstances and situations of his time. An essential step in the renewal of the sacrament of penance is that of our learning to use the scriptural word of God as the voice of Christ which continues to speak.

An example of seeking to bring together the scriptural word and the life of our times to allow the word to speak again can be found in a suggestion of another contemporary writer, the sociologist, Zygmunt Bauman. In the conclusion to his book, *Community*, he refers to the suggestion of another author as follows:

> While the wicked deeds committed 'at the top' inside the offices of big supranational corporations stay as a rule out of sight – and if they appear, fleetingly, in public view are poorly comprehended and paid little attention – public wrath is at its most vicious and vengeful when it comes to harm done to human bodies. Tabogiame (the French name for tobacco addiction), sexual offences and speeding, the three offences most eagerly condemned by public opinion and for which tougher punishment is demanded, are united by nothing other than fears about bodily safety.[15]

These three offences against the body – tobacco smoking, sexual offences and speeding – are interesting! I would suggest that it might be worthwhile to draw these three together with the gospel to allow its light to shine upon them. It is also of interest that the quotation from Bauman draws a contrast between these three offences and 'the wicked deeds committed at the top' which tend to attract less notice.

How do these three offences which arouse social wrath stand up in the light of the account of the Prodigal Son, of the Pharisee and the publican, and of the adulterous woman? How do they compare with the attitudes of those involved in bringing Jesus to his death: Pilate, Caiaphas and the mob?

We need to take note of the things which trigger defensive reactions in our society and in us. But in interplay with the gospel narratives, we have to discern what is at work in such things and do so in the light of what God reveals in the interplays and dialogues of Jesus recorded in the Gospels.

Notes

1. The following works are useful on scapegoating, with more or less reference to Girard: Robert Hammerton-Kelly, *The Gospel and the Sacred* (Minneapolis: Fortress Press, 1994) 129-52; and Raymund

Schwager, *Must There Be Scapegoats?* (New York: Crossroad Publishing Company, 1987) 1-42; James Alison, *Knowing Jesus* (London: SPCK, 1993). For Girard's thought, see René Girard, *I See Satan Fall Like Lightning* (Maryknoll, NY: Orbis Books/ Ottawa: Novalis/ Leominster: Gracewing; 2001) and Michael Kirwan, *Discovering Girard* (London: DLT, 2004).

2. François Bussini, 'L'Intervention de l'assemblée des fedeles au moment de la réconciliation des pénitents d'après les trois 'postulationes' d'un archidiacre romain du Ve-VIe siecle', *Revue de Science Religieuse* 41 (1967) 29-38.

3. Mary C. Mansfield, *The Humiliation of Sinners: Public penance in thirteenth century France* (Ithaca/ London: Cornell University Press, 1995) 177-80.

4. John Dallen, *The Reconciling Community* (New York: Pueblo Publishing Company, 1986) 113-9.

5. See the material on scapegoating in note 1, above.

6. Louis-Marie Chauvet, 'Pratiques pénitentielles et conceptions du péché', *Le Supplement* 120-121 (1977) 41-64; and Jean Charles Payen, 'Le pénitence dans le contexte culturel des XIIe et XIIIe siècles. Des doctrines contritionalistes aux pénitentiels vernaculaires', *Revue des Sciences philosophiques et theologiques* 61 (1977) 399-428.

7. M. F. Berrouard, 'La pénitence publique durant les six premiers siecles: histoire et sociologie', *Maison Dieu* 118 (1974) 92-130.

8. John C. Russell, *The Germanization of Early Medieval Christianity* (New York/ Oxford: Oxford University Press, 1994) 160-1; Peter Brown, *The Rise of Western Christendom* (Cambridge, MA/ Oxford, UK: Blackwells Publishers, 1996) 153-60; Hugh Connolly, *The Irish Penitentials* (Dublin: Four Courts Press, 1995) 162-3.

9. John Bossy, *The Social History of Confession in the Age of the Reformation*. Transactions of the Royal Historical Society, 5th series no. 25 (1975) 21-38; idem, *Christianity in the West 1400-1700* (Oxford/ New York: Oxford University Press,1985) 35-56.

10. Bossy, *Christianity*, 24-6, 33-5; R. Po-Chia Hsia, *The World of Catholic Renewal, 1540-1770* (Cambridge University Press, 1998) 199.

11. Bossy, *Christianity*, 33-5; Roger Chartier, ed. *A History of Private Life*, Vol. III, *Passions of the Renaissance* (Cambridge, MA/ London, England: The Belknap Press of the Harvard University Press, 1989) 59-62, 219-22, 262-3, 512-8, 590-600; Philippe Aries, *Centuries of*

Childhood: A social history of family life (New York: Vintage Press, 1962) 390-400; 403-4, 405-7.

12. See, for example, John Mahoney, *The Making of Moral Theology: A study of the Roman Catholic tradition* (Oxford: The Clarendon Press, 1987).

13. Antoine Vergote, 'Le sacrement de la pénitence et da la réconciliation: Dimensions anthropologiques', *Nouvelle Revue Theologique* 118 (1996) 653-70.

14. ibid., 653.

15. Zygmunt Bauman, *Community: Seeking safety in an insecure world* (Cambridge: Polity Press, 2001) 146.

Chapter 10

Towards the Future of the Sacrament of Penance

As we come to the final chapter of this book, there are four matters I think we need to look at as we seriously consider the future of this sacrament, which future is so tied into the overall re-discovery of our tradition characteristic of this age shaped by the Second Vatican Council, with its call for both a return to the sources and an *aggiornamento*. These four matters are: the great variety and flexibility which the history of this sacrament shows, the specifically sacramental character of the sacrament of penance, the crucial call for a new evangelisation and, finally, the steps that seem to invite us along a path into the future of this sacrament.

Penance: its transitions and shifts

As we have seen in the first part of this book, the history of the sacrament of penance is complex indeed. Its complexity goes beyond that of any of the other sacraments. The sacrament of penance has had several and varied forms and these forms have reflected the successive cultural eras in which the Church has lived.

Every ritual needs to be seen in relationship to the human group to which it belongs; accordingly, we need to see penance as a ritual of the Church. In turn, the Church, like all human groups, needs to be seen within the course of the human history to which it belongs. And we see in all human histories constant cultural modifications and, at times, notable large-scale transitions. We can see the cultural transitions of the Western Church reflected in the history of its use of rites of penance.

The three traditions we have looked at, and the various other rites of penance we have noted, are not isolated rites but articulations of the Church as it has been at various times in its history. These rites grow out of the Church and embody the Church. They embody particular dimensions of the Church's life – those of sin, conversion and forgiveness – and they do this in particular ritual forms. These ritual forms have been open to the continuing influence of new and deeper insights into the Christian tradition and to the mentalities and cultures of their times.

We have seen that these various traditions have arisen and fallen along with the rise and fall of the cultures in which they emerged. We saw that this was so with the first tradition, in the non-use of canonical penance from the late fourth and early fifth centuries because it was no longer practicable for the Christian people; and we saw this in relation to the second tradition, with the felt dissatisfaction of more spiritually aware Christians of the twelfth and thirteenth centuries concerning the penance of the Penitentials which belonged to an earlier time.

This relationship of penance to the eras of the Church's life is important for us as we face the crisis of the sacrament of penance that is occurring today. At the heart of all the change going on in the life of the Church is the fact that we are living in an age of transition in the world at large. One ecclesial culture is passing and another is rising and this is specifically related to the cultural change occurring in the whole of our society today rather than to specific changes or decisions within the Church itself.

The community of the Church always belongs to its surrounding culture, even if that belonging is somewhat different because of its specific identity in Christ. This means that cultural change in the wider society occurs within the Church as well. It sets a new agenda for the Church even though the Church remains always in some way counter-cultural.

Today in so many parts of the world, we are moving from a society which assumed the reality of the religious dimension of human life to one which does not make that socio-structural assumption. This transition has a long history in European cultures and those derived from them; in our times we can see it penetrating right into the mentality of the ordinary people who make up such societies.

This current transition has many dimensions to it. It is not my purpose to go into them all, but it raises questions about many beliefs and practices in the life of the Church. It throws up the very questions of the identity and purpose of the Church, which, in the past, have been taken for granted but which now have again to be explained and justified.

The issues involved in the sacrament of penance today are part of this transition: What is sin? How is sin forgiven? What is our image of God? Is pardon possible? Clearly, if people are not believers, the sacrament can make no sense to them.

As well as this larger social change having its effect within the Church, there has been, since the first half of the twentieth century, a renewal in the understanding of our faith's tradition through such things as the biblical and liturgical renewals, the ecumenical movement and the re-assessment of the history of theology. This has made us look into our tradition more deeply and question many of the ideas, attitudes and practices that have developed or solidified in more recent centuries. The centuries since the Council of Trent need to be seen in the longer perspective offered by the two thousand year length of our tradition.

Looking at our current time, or our recent past, in the light of the whole tradition is a principle of the renewal issuing from the Second Vatican Council. This principle is clearly enunciated by Paul VI in his Introduction to the *General Instruction of the Roman Missal* which responded to a group of prominent Catholics who were questioning the validity of the conciliar reform. Number nine of that documents reads:

> For this reason the 'norm of the Holy Fathers' requires not only the presentation of what our immediate forebears have passed on to us, but also an understanding and a more profound study of the Church's entire past and of all the ways in which her one and only faith has been set forth in the quite diverse human and social forms prevailing in the Semitic, Greek and Latin areas. Moreover, this broader view allows us to see how the Holy Spirit endows the people of God with a marvellous fidelity representing the unalterable deposit of faith, even amid a very great variety of prayers and rites.[1]

Such a study of the Church's entire past has modified our understanding and practice of all the sacraments. Regarding the sacrament of penance, it led the Fathers of Vatican II to make the statement that 'the rite and formulae of Penance are to be revised so that they more clearly express both the nature and effect of the sacrament'.[2] This simple statement is really quite radical in its bluntness.

Thus we can note two aspects of the need for the renewal of the sacrament of penance: first, there is the call for a renewal of the sacrament from within the richness of our own tradition; and, secondly, there is the fact that the whole life of the Church stands at another period of cultural transition such as those in the past which have brought about the rise and fall of the various forms of the sacrament. We need to acknowledge this latter situation, and therefore look to new forms of penance, as well as be aware of the riches which our tradition has to offer in this regard. Part Two of this book has sought to present some strands of the tradition relevant to today's renewal.

This book rests on the presupposition that we are indeed at another transition point in the history of the sacrament of penance which requires us to look for new forms of the sacrament if we are adequately to address what is indeed a lacuna in the current life of the Church: effective rites of conversion.

There will not be an easy or quick solution to this problem. Ready-to-hand solutions were not available in the past; rather, solutions gradually emerged in the midst of considerable discussion and conflict. We will need time, study, reflection and some use of new practices in the process of moving towards a new structuring of rites of penance.

Shifts in the usage of penance

There have been very significant shifts in the usage of the sacrament of penance in the course of its history. It is important to be aware of these in order to give space to our capacity to re-imagine future forms of the sacrament.

First, recall that penance arose in a clearly baptismal matrix: all its elements were derived from the catechumenate which was in a strong process of development in the early Church. In the first form of penance it was as if the penitent went through the catechumenal process which led to baptism again – as if the rite of reconciliation and the re-entry to Eucharist, which concluded the process of penance, replaced the plunging into the baptismal waters and celebration of the Eucharist which brought the baptismal process to its conclusion. In the second and third traditions, this link to baptism became, at best, secondary, at worst, non-existent. The matrix of these later forms was more in the penitential practices of monasticism and especially, in the third tradition, in the use of spiritual direction. Even though both penitential practices and spiritual direction were present in the original baptismal process, they lost their explicit links to it.

So penitential practices moved into a new context, becoming exercises in self-denial without their being seen in their organic relationship to baptism and Eucharist.

They became much more individualist in tone, weakening their innate relationship to the community of the Church expressed in these sacraments. And the third tradition, especially in its beginnings, was seen more as an element of the individual's journey to holiness.

A second significant shift in the usage of the sacrament of penance concerned the nature of the sins for which the sacrament was to be used. We saw that its original use was only for very serious sin: idolatry, murder, adultery. This list was expanded in later uses of the first tradition. But in the Penitentials there was a much expanded list of sins for which it was used. However, as time went on, the sacrament came in practice to be used only for the sins of the very devout; we saw such usage with Caesarius of Arles, who recommended that it not be used by the greater number of people. It was also the more devout who used this rite in the beginnings of the third tradition: confession. A different and difficult situation then arose with the Fourth Lateran Council's imposition of the annual use of the sacrament by all Catholics. In the twentieth century, the sacrament was used for all sins and, practically speaking, it came to be the only way that forgiveness was seen to be given.

A third shift concerns the temporal dimension of the sacrament. Originally, the sacrament involved several years' duration to complete it – in imitation of the catechumenate. In Irish penance it took an indeterminate time but, given the penances required, it would have involved considerable time. On the other hand, the third tradition, as it developed, especially in the twentieth century, made the duration required for the sacrament only a few minutes.

This third shift is tied into a fourth: that of the emphasis placed on the various elements of the sacrament. The outstanding element of both exclusion and Irish penance was that of doing penances: prayers, fasting, self-denial, physical penances. This is what took up the time and continuing attention of the penitent. It was the substance of the performance of the sacrament. In the confession tradition, on the other hand, the penances became less and less significant as time went on, the emphasis shifting to, at first, the penitent's interior state of contrition and, later, to the priest's absolution.

A fifth shift of considerable importance concerns the frequency with which the sacrament could be used. As we have seen, there was a very strict understanding in the early centuries that this sacrament could be used only once, just as baptism could be received only once. Yet in the confession tradition of the sacrament, it can be used as often as the penitent requests it. Some people have desired a daily use of the sacrament.

A final, but by no means insignificant, sixth shift focuses on the foundational issue of how conversion is understood. In earlier centuries there was a broader understanding of the Church's overall life of conversion in which our daily sins and weaknesses were seen as forgiven by our turning to God in prayer and, indeed, by simply living a Christian life. St Augustine stated that such sins are forgiven every time we pray the Lord's Prayer. As an extension of this, great importance was given to those times in the Church's life of prayer which emphasised conversion; Lent was the classic example of such a time. The more specific rites of penance were reserved for the greater sins. There has been a shift from this situation to one in which, practically speaking, the sacrament of penance is seen as the basic way of dealing with all sin. This latter situation has been particularly true in the centuries following the Reformation in which 'going to confession' became one of the distinctive marks of being a Catholic.

All these shifts indicate not only a wide variety of rites in the history of the sacrament but considerable shifts in its spirit; they illustrate a constant adaptability to new situations as they arise. Forms of penance used in one particular era of the Church's life would be close to being unrecognisable by Catholics of other eras!

Our recent tradition and the future

The recently inherited form of the sacrament of penance which we have called confession cannot be seen as representative, much less as normative, for the future. It has much that is important and precious in it which we must take with us into the future but it represents only one period in the overall Catholic tradition and we must see it within that tradition.

Both Part One of this book, in its five chapters dealing with the history of this sacrament, and the preceding section, on the shifts in its usage, alert us to the fact that this sacrament has been open to great variation and has shown itself to be very adaptable in response to historically significant changes in circumstances.

Before we are genuinely able to begin to dialogue about this sacrament and to celebrate it well we need to soak up this history and the circumstances that have shaped it. I say this believing, as previously stated, that we stand at another of these transition points in our history which have so shaped this sacrament.

It has been my purpose to emphasise the specific character of each of the traditions of penance. As a consequence, the uniqueness of each of them, and the differences and discontinuities between them, have come out. There are of course also real continuities between them: each of them deals with sin, penance and reconciliation. Each of them deals with contrition, the acknowledgment of sin, the healing of sinfulness and its effects, prayer, self-denial, and the expression of God's forgiveness in an act of reconciliation or absolution. A transformation of these various elements goes on across the traditions; they are integrated in different ways in each of them. As we seek a new form, or forms, for expressing the Church's life of conversion, we need to be aware of these elements and seek to assume them in new ways into future rites of penance.

Penance is a sacrament

The title of this section may seem to state the obvious but it is crucial to take proper account of the fact that penance is a sacrament and that, as a consequence, it is part of the Church's organic sacramental system. Such a title articulates a particular dimension of the Church's life as a communion of life in Christ. This is an essential point in the re-thinking of the sacrament and in composing new forms for its celebration.

As we have seen, it took some time for penance consistently to be named as one of the seven sacraments. This happened only as part of a general redescription of the sacraments in conjunction with the process of distinguishing the seven sacraments from the other rites of the Church.

We have also seen that there was some awareness of differences of sacramental status between the different medieval rites of penance. We saw such prominent medieval theologians as Peter Lombard and Albert the Great attributing a greater sacramental status to the rites of public penance than to those of private penance (see Ch. 4, n. 3). The greater antiquity and the irrepeatable character of public penance gave it, in their view, a greater sacramental status.

I think there is something important tucked away in the comments of these theologians. They were aware that the private penance that was on the rise in their time was a recent thing and was quite different from the ancient traditional rites which were still used in particular circumstances.

I would like to bounce off an opinion from those medieval theologians and suggest that the sacrament of penance in its later traditions has been loosed from some of its moorings in the sacramental system. It is not quite anchored as it ought to be. Like Lombard and Albert, we may need to reflect on some of the deficiencies of later rites of penance in the light of the origins of the sacrament. It has often been the case in the history of the Church that a return to our sources has lighted the way into the future. This we have seen at work in the Second Vatican Council.

As we have also seen, the origin of the sacrament of penance is baptismal. It is explicitly formed out of baptismal 'raw materials' and is given its own specific climax with the reconciliation of the penitent to the eucharistic community, just as baptism reaches its climax with the entry of the newly baptised into the eucharistic community. This reference to baptism has been lost in the liturgical rite of the sacrament and, consequently, in the felt experience of the penitent – and that of the confessor. This is important, given that the sacraments are ritual acts which do what they signify. In its celebration, penance does not show its roots in baptism or its orientation to the Eucharist. Theologically, we can elaborate an understanding of penance which links it to these other two sacraments but in its ritual performance it does not do so explicitly.

Penance is not just a spiritual discipline or a moral practice but a sacrament, and the dynamics which ought to be at work in it are the dynamics of a sacrament and of the sacramental life of the Church. Our considerations regarding the sacrament of penance in the past have taken place in the spheres of moral and spiritual theology more so than within the sphere of sacramental theology.

Penance is an exercise of our baptismal plunging into Christ celebrated because we see that the journey upon which our baptism has set us includes the continuing presence of sin in us and around us. That journey requires us to renew the source of our life given in baptism, as it also requires the renewal of our baptismal commitment.

Penance is a return to 'the spring of living water' who is Christ in order to be re-invigorated for the journey to which we are committed. Penance is a return to the Christ who baptised us and calls us to conversion. Its celebration needs baptismal imagery.

Penance is oriented to the celebration of the Eucharist, which is the sacrament of reconciliation par excellence. Theologically, the relationship of the priest's absolution to the Eucharist in the practice of recent centuries is parallel to the relationship, in the ancient Order of Public Penance, between the Preface, in which the penitent's reconciliation is proclaimed and expressed, and the Eucharist which followed it. The Preface was part of the traditional rite for the reconciliation of public penitents on Holy Thursday morning. At this Mass on Holy Thursday, the bishop reconciled the public penitents. Penance has its natural point of arrival in the Eucharist, as does baptism. The celebration of penance needs eucharistic references.

In what I am saying here about the relationship between penance and baptism, on the one hand, and penance and Eucharist, on the other, it is very important to grasp the principles involved, whatever may or may not be possible for us in our practice at the moment.

As a sacrament, penance is a celebration of Christ's death and resurrection and the imagery of that paschal mystery needs to pervade it and not just be laid on top of a practice with which it does not naturally fit. As a liturgical celebration it needs to give body to that imagery, along with the imagery of the gospel parables of forgiveness. The General Introduction of the *Rite of Penance* of 1973 is a good start on this as it presents the sacrament in these fundamental terms. The formula of absolution in that same rite likewise presents the sacrament as a celebration of Christ's death and resurrection. Our rites need to be renewed by reference to this mystery so that they may 'more clearly express the nature and effect of the sacrament'.

As a sacrament, penance is not just an act done by the Church, but it sacramentalises the Church; it gives form to the Church in one of its dimensions; it articulates that dimension of the Church's nature and life. This sacrament came into the life of the Church as the Church took stronger cognisance of the fact that it is sinful yet holy; that it lives in the eschatological tension between being 'already' in union with Christ and, consequently, holy, on the one hand, and being 'not yet' in union with Christ, and so sinful, on the other. To say this another way: we are already in communion with Christ but this communion is yet to penetrate and possess us and will not do so until the Lord's coming is complete and all things are made new.

It was in the conflicts with the purists of the early centuries who refused to have a sacrament of penance for those who had seriously sinned after baptism that the Church came to increasing clarity about her sinful yet holy state.

Thus this sacrament articulates the life of the Church as caught in the tension between 'now' and 'the future' and, so, as a sinful yet holy Church: the Church that St Augustine describes as a 'chaste prostitute'. This tension cannot be resolved: it will always be part of the Church's life until the Lord's coming is fulfilled. It is part of the essential context for a Christian understanding of both sin and conversion.

The sacrament of conversion

There is a very practical consequence of the centrality of the paschal mystery for the sacrament of penance. Forgiveness is given; it flows from 'the spring of living water' from which springs all of our life in Christ. I would suggest that it is not quite to the point to describe penance as the sacrament of forgiveness but rather that it would be more accurate to describe it as the sacrament of conversion.

The forgiveness of God is poured out upon us through Christ's death and resurrection. But are our hearts open to that forgiveness? Are they turned towards it? Or are they occupied elsewhere? This sacrament is the sacrament of conversion, of turning to God, of making that shift involved in going beyond our minds, as the biblical notion of conversion implies in the Greek word, *metanoia*, used in the Gospels. It means going beyond our present way of seeing things, and taking up the way proposed by the gospel of Christ.

We do not have to earn or merit God's forgiveness. We receive it.

The sacrament of penance sacramentalises conversion, our turning to the God of reconciliation and forgiveness. It seeks to give symbolic or sacramental form to our return to God, imaged for us in the return of the Prodigal Son, in the freeing of the adulterous woman, in the simple faith in God's mercy of the publican at the back of the Temple, and in the words and attitude of the good thief who turns to Jesus and asks to be remembered by him.

The history of the sacrament in its first two traditions makes clear that we are dealing with the sacrament of conversion. The substance of the sacrament in both those traditions was the doing of prayer, penance and fasting as means of conversion of heart, as ways in which the sinful heart was re-attuned to God. What these rites sought to bring about was the turning of the person to God. These came to their climax in the first tradition in a rite of reconciliation leading to communion with God in Christ in the Eucharist. The rite is not complete without the climax in the act of reconciliation because the purpose of conversion is greater communion with God. It seeks to allow that communion to further penetrate and possess us as God's work of conversion in us seeks to remove the obstacles to that communion.

Conversion (repentance) and reconciliation are two moments of the one process, each having their own specific emphasis. In conversion, reconciliation is already occurring; in reconciliation, conversion is effected.

The sequence for the reception of the sacraments

Renewing the sacrament of penance specifically as a sacrament, and seeing it within the overall sacramental structure of the Church's life, leads us to unearth aspects of it which have been occluded by the emphases incorporated into its later historical forms.

I would suggest that one of the most fruitful things that such a re-orientation would lead to would be a repositioning of penance in the sequence of sacraments into which people are initiated. In the light of its origin, I would suggest that, for persons baptised as infants, it ought to be received after the completion of Christian initiation, which takes place in the first full celebration of the Eucharist by the first reception of Communion.

Once we see penance as sourced in baptism, as deepening and furthering our baptismal commitment to conversion, it is then logical to celebrate it after the completion of baptism in Eucharist. Once we acknowledge the original parallel between baptism's climaxing in Eucharist and penance's climaxing in Eucharist, then it makes sense to celebrate penance after the completion of Christian initiation in Eucharist.

This requires a re-conception of penance in terms of its sacramentality and, specifically, in terms of its relationship to baptism and Eucharist. In this connection, it makes sense for us to go back to our sources to seek there our way ahead. In this of course we do not wish to go back to a past stage of the history of penance but rather to find in an earlier stage of our tradition the wherewithal to move on into the future. This is a strategy that we use whenever we get into an impasse in the history of the tradition. In the twentieth century we did this with many strands of our tradition, as is attested by the renewal surrounding Vatican II.

In making this suggestion I am not recommending that we ought to privilege the first stage of our tradition to the detriment of later stages. They all have their part to play in the complex weaving of the tradition and we need to approach all stages critically. However there is a uniqueness about the first stage of any branch of the tradition in that it provides an orientation to that line of the tradition. It acts as the launching pad for that branch, distinguishing it from other branches of the tradition. It does have, therefore, a particular dignity and should attract particular notice in reflection on the tradition. Thus, in dealing with any particular theological topic, we attend first of all to what the New Testament has to say about it.

The suggestion above – that the sacrament of penance needs to be re-located in the sequence of reception of the sacraments – is made on theological grounds, but it would also be pastorally more effective.

In the present way of things we often seek to use confirmation in later childhood or adolescence as a form of renewal of faith or, if you like, as a renewal of baptism. In doing this, we are trying to make 'a silk purse out of a sow's ear'. Confirmation as a sacrament cannot do it. It is not about the renewal of baptism but a stage of the baptismal process which has become loosed from its moorings within that process because of particular historical circumstances in the Western Church. Sacraments are supposed to do what they say; they are not subject to our desire to make of them what we want them to be.

Looking at penance in relationship to baptism and Eucharist, however, enables us to see that penance is precisely a way of renewing our baptism. It is what we so often seek to force confirmation to be. Penance is the renewal of baptism; in that was its origin. So is penance not the best means at our disposal to use as baptismal renewal, as renewal, that is, in the Christian life?

This proposal involves a different form of renewal of baptism from that expressed in the original form of penance which took place against the background of sins so serious that they seemed to have vitiated the original baptismal commitment and thus required people to go through the baptismal process again as second penance or a second conversion. But given the history of this sacrament in all its variety, which shows such great malleability of form and spirit by which it has been adapted to so many different mentalities and circumstances, I would suggest that a new form of the sacrament of penance could be created out of the raw materials embodied in the tradition. This would serve both as a sacramental baptismal renewal, at a time chosen for its appropriateness, and as an introduction to the lifelong use of this sacrament in the several forms offered in such a new structuring of rites.

This would be quite different from attempts to use confirmation for such a renewal because penance is about conversion whereas confirmation is not. Penance is in the right dimension of the Church's life.

I can imagine that this proposal might seem to some people like turning a renewal program into a sacrament and so it could be misinterpreted as undermining the importance and dignity of the sacrament. I would respond to this by saying that people who practised the rites of penance according to the various strands of the tradition would have found the rites of other strands insufficient and misplaced in regard to their own. So, for example, people who saw exclusion penance as the Church's rite of penance saw the rise of tariff penance as the rise of something quite unacceptable and, indeed, in the opinion of some, as an abomination. To see the legitimacy of this proposal would require us to rethink our recently received tradition so as to allow us to see the sacramentality of such a rite. Such a rethinking has happened in the life of the Church before, as we have seen.

The understandings of conversion in each of the three historical traditions are somewhat different. The different 'flavours' which the words 'conversion', 'repentance' and 'penance' have taken on in the course of their histories resonates with these differences. Even though such words as 'conversion' and the others were very close in their original meanings, they have taken on different shades of meaning over time. 'Conversion', particularly as understood in terms of the New Testament Greek word, *metanoia*, has greater breadth and depth to it. It has a profoundly positive dimension, especially when seen as leading into the following of Jesus.

If we take the word 'conversion' in this richer sense, the sacrament of conversion in which it is expressed also takes on a richer meaning so that the new structure of the sacrament that I am suggesting here would take in this broader and richer understanding of conversion as a passover into communion with Christ and out of the sinfulness which impedes that communion.

I do not wish to suggest that such use of the sacrament of penance should be the only use of the sacrament in the life of the Church. The particular value of such an opportunity for a formal sacramental renewal of baptism through such 'an entry into penance' would be as the way in which people would be introduced to the use of the sacrament in whatever forms it might have.

Given the relationship of penance to baptism and to Eucharist and given an understanding of penance as conversion, as that is understood by the Gospels, the sacrament would offer a renewal of the whole of the Christian life.

There is another pastoral advantage to this proposal and that is that it provides an opportunity to look at Christian life and conversion at an age in the lifespan at which it would be more appropriate to consider the real issues of Christian conversion than is at present the case in the pastoral practice of the Church, where quite young children (baptised as infants) are introduced to the sacrament of penance.

Penance and a new evangelisation

In looking to the future of the sacrament of penance, we need to take account of a far-reaching pastoral call by recent popes. In the documents related to the new millennium and the holy year which celebrated it, John Paul II called for a new evangelisation. He had also taken up this topic in an earlier document of 1990, *Redemptoris Missio*, on the missionary activity of the Church.

These documents often fall back upon an earlier document of Paul VI on the theme of evangelisation, called *Evangelii Nuntiandi*. This had been published in 1975. The importance of this document has again been brought to light recently through the many celebrations of its thirtieth anniversary, in 2005.

Evangelisation, conversion and the sacrament of penance are closely inter-related because it is the proclamation of the gospel which gives rise to true Christian conversion, as we see right from the earliest accounts of the proclamation of the gospel in the New Testament.

The call for a new evangelisation by John Paul II and, earlier, the call for 'a new period of evangelisation' by Paul VI,[3] are fundamental responses on the parts of both popes to the new age in which we are living. Together, their calls comprise a profound recognition of the Church's passing out of an earlier age of its history, based on an earlier evangelisation, to a new age in which, again, we must proclaim the word of God which, by the power of the Spirit, keeps the Church alive.

The documents relating to evangelisation by both John Paul II and Paul VI make it clear that evangelisation involves the evangelisation of human cultures. Paul VI says:

... what matters is to evangelise man's [*sic*] culture and cultures (not in a purely decorative way, as it were, by applying a thin veneer, but in a vital way, in depth and right to their very roots), in the wide and rich sense which those words have in *Gaudium et Spes*.[4]

One consequence of evangelisation being the evangelisation of cultures is that, with the changing of human cultures, there is occasioned the need for a renewal of evangelisation appropriate to the new culture. Thus, in our age of cultural transition, we face this need for a new evangelisation of human beings and the culture in which, and according to which, they live out their lives.

Along with this goes the reality that evangelisation is never complete. The Church – and not only the world – is always in need of evangelisation; it will not be complete until the Lord manifests himself in glory to make all things new. We are always living in this time in which Christ's work is achieved 'already but not yet'; the evangelisation of believers themselves has to continue. To quote Paul VI again:

[The Church] needs to listen unceasingly to what she must believe, to her reasons for hoping, to the new commandment of love. She is the People of God immersed in the world, and often tempted by idols, and she always needs to hear the proclamation of the 'mighty works of God' which converted her to the Lord, she always needs to be called together afresh by him and reunited. In brief, this means that she has a constant need of being evangelised, if she wishes to retain freshness, vigour and strength in order to proclaim the gospel.[5]

So there are two levels to this new evangelisation: the realisation that we must always be evangelised and the particular need for a new evangelisation in our time because of its particular character as a period of cultural transition.

Evangelisation is the proclaiming of the gospel of Jesus Christ, wherever that occurs and however that occurs. It is not containable or masterable.[6] It involves the explicit proclamation of the gospel, the witness of the life of believers, the influence of the Christian family, the life of the community of faith, Christian service etc. It is, as Paul VI says, very complex, and we cannot reduce it to any partial or fragmentary definition.[7] As part of the complex whole, there is the essential element of the explicit proclamation of Jesus the Christ as himself the Good News.

This evangelisation is about the 'making new' of humanity, that is, the renewing of individual persons and the whole of humankind. Paul VI hangs his words on a quotation from the book of Revelation: 'Now I am making the whole of creation new' (Rev 21:5).[8]

Evangelii Nuntiandi gives a wonderful description of how this happens. Evangelisation, this renewing power of the gospel, seeks to bring 'the good news into all the strata of humanity'.[9] The document goes on to delineate what these various strata of humanity are:

> The strata of humanity which are transformed: for the Church it is a question not only of preaching the gospel in ever wider geographic areas or to ever greater numbers of people, but also of affecting and as it were upsetting, through the power of the gospel, mankind's [*sic*] criteria of judgement, determining values, points of interest, lines of thought, sources of inspiration and models of life, which are in contrast with the word of God and the plan of salvation.[10]

This list of the strata of humanity gives us an insight into the depths of our individual and cultural being that the gospel seeks to reach and make new by bringing them to conversion.

Evangelisation releases the power of God's Spirit in us, that same Spirit who was at work in Jesus to bring about in us the new humankind which we have seen in him. The importance of the above quotation from Paul VI is that in the list of the strata of humanity to be affected by the gospel, he gives us a chance to see how deeply the word of God seeks to affect and, where necessary, upset us. This is not just a matter of how we think or what we feel; it is neither simply doctrinal nor emotional but seeks to affect those things which make us the sort of human beings that we are. It asks us to look into the depths of ourselves and to discern what is really at work in us. This list of the strata of humanity – 'criteria of judgement, determining values, points of interest, lines of thought, sources of inspiration, models of life' – takes us beyond our immediate thoughts, attitudes, feelings and actions to see what shapes them, what structures our thoughts, feelings, attitudes and behaviour at a deeper level. It is thus that we uncover our innate criteria of judgment etc.

This takes us back to Chapter Eight of this book, entitled *Conversion: Living in memory of Christ.* In that chapter we saw that conversion involves a shift from living in memory of our human past as that is packed into us and as we live it out knowingly or unknowingly, to living in memory of Jesus, as we come into contact with him through the tradition we live and, more specifically, through the Scriptures. What we described in that chapter in terms of memory can also be understood by looking at the presumed strata of our humanity that are at work in us and in our inherited human situation. The transition to living in memory of Jesus – which, we remember, was compared to migration in that chapter – is a shift into the transformed strata of the new humanity lived by Jesus.

There is at work in this evangelisation an 'affecting', even an 'upsetting', of these strata of humanity. The gospel, as we have seen, offers us the possibility of a shift in perspective; it changes our 'take' on human life. So the proclamation of Christ's death and resurrection changes our perspective on the whole stretch of human life, opening us up to the future of our life given to us in that resurrection out of death. But it is not just a message about the end of life: it is about the nature of our life as we live it now as stretching further into life through death.

This new perspective, this new 'model of life' given by the gospel, makes a Christian view of life different from that of a person who sees death as the end or from one who does not see life as a gift coming to us from God's hand. Such a different view of life relates not simply to living morally or otherwise. Rather, such a view of life has practical, lived consequences in terms of thoughts, attitudes, feelings and actions or in terms of 'criteria of judgement, determining values, points of interest, lines of thought, sources of inspiration, models of life'. From the perspective that the gospel of Jesus gives us, we may see such thoughts, attitudes, feelings, actions etc. as being for the good, or the ill, of humanity and we are impelled to bear witness to our views, while respecting the views of those who see things differently.

Evangelisation and penance

The importance of dealing with this question of evangelisation in relation to the sacrament of penance lies firstly in the fact, stated earlier, that it is the proclamation of the gospel (evangelisation) which gives rise to conversion. Conversion follows evangelisation; it does not precede it. This conversion is of a particular character, as we have seen in Chapter Six of this book, which dealt with the Scriptures and their role in the Christian life. The proclamation of the gospel, when it takes root in human beings, upsets those internal strata of our humanity which are out of tune with it.

In fact, we are not dealing with a genuine sense of sin unless the light of God's word has led directly or indirectly to its discovery. In Christian conversion we are not dealing specifically with what our surrounding society sees either as wrong or as what is the 'done thing' but with what the light of the word of God pinpoints as out of tune with God, as revealed in Jesus. Seeing this sacrament in terms of our compliance with a set of commandments, even the Ten Commandments, is not sufficient since it is not adequately grounded in the character of Christian conversion. This conversion works at the level of 'the strata of humanity' spoken about by Pope Paul VI, which involves much more than mere compliance with a law code.

The question of the need for a new evangelisation, as presented by Paul VI and John Paul II, secondly, points up the fact that we are entering a new era in the Church's life in which we need to proclaim the gospel anew in those parts of the world which were formerly considered evangelised. This is tied into the period of cultural change which has became obvious in our time. Such 'post-Christian' cultures no longer carry the gospel within their structures and ethos in such a way that they can be instruments of evangelisation, as formerly they were. They can no longer communicate the values of the gospel to their members as once they did.

Cultural transitions have in the past been associated with the rise and fall of various forms of the sacrament of penance and, as I have several times suggested, the underlying reason for the present malaise concerning the sacrament of penance is tied into the cultural transition happening now.

The understanding of the depths which the gospel seeks to reach in human beings, and which is presented in *Evangelii Nuntiandi* and *Redemptoris Missio*, has consequences for the way we see conversion. Conversion in this light is about the strata of humanity with which the word of God seeks to deal. What is true of conversion is true of its sacrament. We require forms of the sacrament able to deal with these strata of humanity. Conversion cannot happen unless the word of God is effectively proclaimed and we provide the means by which it can complete its course within us. As stated earlier on, the renewal of the sacrament of penance is simply an application of the renewal of our understanding and use of the scriptural word of God.

One of the elements of the tradition which has been extremely influential in shaping the forms of the sacrament is the legal framework within which the sacrament has so often been conceived. By this I do not just mean legalism as an exaggeration of the legal, but the legal itself. This has involved, as just mentioned, celebrating the sacrament in terms of the Ten Commandments and the commandments of the Church.

There have been various metaphors at work in the understanding and practice of the sacrament, such as those of healing and of spiritual direction. I think, however, that the metaphor which has become the core metaphor in both theology and practice is that of the law and the courtroom. Sin has been thought of in legal terms, the role of the priest in terms of being a judge, the acts of penance or satisfaction in terms of making satisfaction in a legal sense or as punishment. The image of God has been that of a judge – even if as a merciful and loving judge, the legal image still remained. Without denying other metaphors, or the influence of insightful and sensitive confessors or the desire of penitents to progress spiritually, I believe that we can say that the law and its imagery have provided the major metaphor for this sacrament.

I hope that this book has shown the inadequacy of this metaphor. I would go further and suggest that it is in fact an impediment to the use of the sacrament in our time, given the greater awareness we have, for instance, of the imagery of redemption, and so of God, that our tradition in its greater depth presents.

The very rediscovery of the tradition undermines such legal imagery. However, we are also dealing with a new way of thinking about our own humanity. Our thoughts about what shapes human beings are much more influenced by psychology and allied sciences. This cannot be ignored; rather we must work with this rising understanding of what it is to be a human being in order to evangelise in our own era. This is where that remarkable passage of *Evangelii Nuntiandi* dealing with the strata of humanity comes in. In that list we have an approach to our humanity which lends itself to a richer understanding of what we are seeking to do in the sacrament of penance. Looking at that list: 'criteria of judgement, determining values, points of interest, lines of thought, sources of inspiration and models of life', we have several different ways offered to us of dealing with the basic orientation of our lives. Christianity offers a different model of life from consumerism, atheism, false religiosity and individualism. In each of these views of human life, there is embedded a model of life involving 'criteria of judgement, determining values, points of interest, lines of thought and sources of inspiration'.

In dialoguing with the Scriptures, most especially the Gospels, we can find ways in which the various models of life that are within us are affected and upset, just as we see that happening between Jesus and those with whom he is in dialogue in the Scriptures.

I am suggesting that these strata of our humanity which indicate the level at which the gospel seeks to affect us can provide a guide for the development of a new model of the sacrament of penance, a new framework within which to celebrate the sacrament, just as the legal framework gave us a paradigm in the past.

This leads me to say yet again that the renewal of the sacrament of penance cannot be achieved quickly or simply by the introduction of new rites or a return to old ones, but requires time, thought and the prudent use of rites attuned to contemporary cultures.

Towards the renewal the sacrament of penance

In other periods of change in the Church's use of rites of penance, a new practice has never arisen quickly or easily. It has always taken time and involved diversity and even conflicts. We have seen such things in the rise to prominence of the three main traditions of the sacrament and things will prove to be similar in our times. We will, I believe, gradually work towards a renewed theology and a renewed practice both of which will show continuity and discontinuity with past theology and practice.

I have deliberately spoken in terms of moving 'towards a theology and practice of penance' because that is where we need to locate our present situation and this book.

The understanding of this sacrament is an integral part of the continuing re-discovery of the history of the Christian tradition and the consequent renewal of theology going on in our times. In regard to this sacrament it involves especially a theology: of the Scriptures; of the redemption; of sin, including original sin; and of the nature of sacramentality. It is also closely linked to an understanding of the relationship between psychology, morality and the gospel – Christian morality has always had close links with the thought of its time. This sacrament is particularly sensitive to the predominant imagery of the faith used at particular times and in particular cultures.

It also needs to be said that we need this sacrament. Conversion and a sacramental means of celebrating and deepening it are crucial to the life of the Church. There is no Christian discipleship without conversion.

This, however, is no argument to continue the practices of the immediate past; rather, it is a stimulus to find practices which are effective in our culture and time. One of the negative aspects of the history of this sacrament is a recurrent loss of pastoral appropriateness and hence of practical application. This we saw in the first tradition:

once the Church became a Church of larger numbers in the fourth century, the old practice of exclusion penance no longer proved practicable and fell into disuse. Leaders of the Church recommended its use be delayed! It became largely a deathbed practice. Similarly, the Irish system proved too onerous and provoked the rise of the understandable strategies of commutation and redemption to enable the penances to be done within a reasonable time. The confession tradition worked well for an elite of believers but, once imposed on all Catholics, considerable pastoral difficulties arose which made the sacrament a burden; it asked of ordinary people and pastors skills that neither had. In our times, with a much more aware and critical laity, the need to attend to this question of the pastoral aptness of our rites of penance has again become acute.

There has, at times, been a niggardliness to the Church's practice which is in contrast to the readiness to receive and pardon sinners, as seen in the gospel narratives.

We need this sacrament and we need forms of it which are effective among the people of God. To be effective, we have to take today's situation into account as that forms part of the mentality of the people of God. We should do this both to be able to pass on the tradition today and to know those elements of the current mentality to which we need to take a counter-cultural position in order to live out the tradition genuinely.

Without being able to give an exhaustive account of today's mentality, I think that the points quoted in the previous chapter, from the article of Anton Vergote, are worth keeping in mind as general indicators of the mentality with which we are dealing. He makes several points of great relevance. First, the natural religiosity of the past, with its sense of duty towards God, has disappeared and been replaced by a sense of duty towards others. This has become part of the Western mentality and we cannot ignore it when dealing with the sacrament of penance. Secondly, the more individual morality, with special sensitivity to sexual questions, has given way to a more collective mentality especially sensitive to social (and ecological) questions. Thirdly, psychological techniques to overcome personal difficulties and faults have come to predominate over the acknowledgment of sin before God. Fourthly, a tendency has arisen to see Christian morality as a general morality having no specific character of its own. Fifthly, there is a strong sense of human autonomy which sees individual conscience as the arbiter of all; this can tend to sideline Christian formation of conscience and any reference to the Church or the tradition. And sixthly, Vergote argues that the interiorisation of the faith is the only real basis for the effective celebration of the sacrament of penance. This point of course is true for the whole Church today.

With the exception of his sixth point, each of the points that Vergote makes contains positive and negative elements with regard to the sacrament of penance. For instance, in relation to the first point, the loss of a sense of God does not help in making sense of this sacrament but the sense of duty to one's neighbour is a great positive in regard to the gospel and this sacrament; it can even help avoid some of our misplaced actions of the past. In connection with the second point, the greater attention to the communal and to social questions is a positive thing for the gospel and the sacrament. Thirdly, the psychological sciences can indeed be a great help in naming the true nature of sin and the sources of negative actions in people's lives without taking over from the specific naming of sin and the call to live the gospel. Fourthly, there is much in common between Christian morality and other moralities but, as has been often insisted on in this book, there is a very specific character to Christian morality which needs to be clarified and insisted on. Fifthly, we do indeed have to honour what Cardinal Newman called 'Pope Conscience'; yet, to neglect the proper formation of conscience is to open ourselves to the small – and large – terrors of which human beings are capable of unleashing.

These points of Vergote seem to me to pinpoint major difficulties in renewing the sacrament of penance, and they highlight the fact that more than minor adjustments or greater moral urging are required precisely because we are dealing with a major change of mentality and culture. They particularly show that our practice needs to be specifically Christian practice based particularly on the scriptural word of God. Our practice can no longer fall back on a generally accepted cultural mentality; therefore interiorisation of the faith is indeed necessary.

In renewing the understanding and practice of the sacrament, let us also keep in mind the following points whose importance we have seen in the course of this book. First, at the risk of being tiresome, we must emphasise again that the sacrament cannot be celebrated adequately without the celebration of God's word in terms of the understanding of the role of the scriptural word as seen above. The proclamation and reception of that word is embodied in the celebration of the sacrament.

Secondly, this sacrament is about conversion, not just about forgiveness; it is about the change of heart that conversion, in the gospel sense of that word, implies. 'Conversion' is a much more helpful word than 'penance' because it resonates more with the meaning of the word *metanoia* used in the New Testament. It is helpful to use the word 'conversion' to describe the sacrament. Describing the sacrament too narrowly, just in terms of forgiveness, without seeing its link to conversion, can render the sacrament meaningless.

Thirdly, the spirit of conversion in us is God at work in us already showing his forgiveness at work in us; it is his reconciling presence in us. This was insisted on by the tradition leading from Abelard to and beyond St Thomas

Aquinas. This was so strong in their thought that St Thomas in particular felt keenly the need to explain adequately the purpose of the priest's absolution. The whole process being given form in the sacrament is the action of God in us; it is not something we do to bring about God's forgiveness. The sacrament embodies the movement in the heart of the publican at the back of the Temple, not that of the Pharisee at the front of the Temple.

Fourthly, we need to recognise that our tradition sees the purpose of the major rites of penance as applying to serious sin rather than to lesser, daily or venial sins. This is true not only of the first tradition but clearly also of the third. We have seen that both St Augustine and St Thomas were clear on this, as was the Council of Trent, which stated that it is not necessary to confess venial sins to the priest because they can be forgiven in many different ways.[11] Thus we need to acknowledge explicitly the many ways in which our general sinfulness is forgiven and not be afraid to use rites specifically designed for the forgiveness of the general, daily sinful acts that are part of the lives of the whole people of God. Such rites range from the penitential rite at Mass to the specific, communal rites of penance that we may use at important times of the year.

Along with this we need to acknowledge that there are moments in peoples' lives when their following of Christ is in genuine jeopardy, when they do make choices by which they withdraw themselves from God and his ways. These situations of serious sin need to be dealt with in an adequate way in rites oriented to such situations. Such situations need individual attention.

We do indeed need a range of rites for this sacrament. We have a range of rites in the 1973 *Rite of Penance*, but they are too constrained by the recent past of the Church's tradition to be able to meet the current situation as they are.

The immediate future

By means of the fundamental strategy of looking at the present situation of the sacrament of penance in the light of earlier periods of its history and, particularly, its times of transition, this book is looking towards the future of the sacrament. In doing this I am interpreting the present situation of the sacrament in terms of the demise of one form of penance in expectation of the rise of another form. The 1973 *Rite of Penance* could be seen as the rise of that new form but in fact it has not gained a foothold in either the practice or the mentality of the Church. It suffers, as said immediately above, by being under the shadow of the Church's recent practice which is in need of reform. This 1973 *Rite* does provide good steps ahead and truly helpful perspectives which have been noted in the course of this book.

As noted earlier, we cannot expect truly effective immediate results regarding this sacrament because the building blocks of the new practice are not yet sufficiently in place. These concern not just the liturgy of penance or its theology but the overall movement of theological and pastoral renewal going on in the Church and the cultural shift through which we are living at this time.

So we are dealing not just with the forms that the sacrament might take but also with its spirit and theology. This sacrament is a celebration of the paschal mystery, of Christ's death and resurrection in which sin and death are overcome. This sacrament is about the victorious love of God which raises Jesus out of the death imposed on him by the sinfulness of humanity and which robs sinfulness of its power. We have been set free from sin. Despite its continuing presence and power among us, we can 'laugh in its face' because it no longer has the power to separate us from God. In this sacrament we place ourselves as sinners into the hands of the Father who redeems us, who buys us out of slavery.

The sacrament is in no way an earning of God's forgiveness nor is it a gaining of forgiveness we don't already have; it is the entrusting of ourselves as sinners into the hands of the God who has already forgiven us in Christ in the face of further evidence of our sinfulness. We are forgiven sinners.

This sacrament is a sacrament of faith, of faith in the fact that God has already forgiven us and set us free. We are always subject to the desire to overcome our sinfulness ourselves rather than to entrust ourselves to God, as the gospel insists and the sacrament celebrates. This constant entrusting of ourselves into God's hands is what brings about our liberation from sin. The sacrament needs to be permeated with this spirit of the paschal mystery as both the absolution formula and the Introduction of the 1973 *Rite* clearly show.

The original meaning of the word, 'confession', captures this paschal spirit. The word has come to mean 'naming our sins' in recent centuries. In the Scriptures and the earlier writings of the Church, it meant, rather, 'to recognise or acknowledge' and so the prayer of confession was a prayer of recognition of the goodness of God often against the background of our sinfulness. St Augustine's *Confessions* is a prayer in which he recognises the goodness of God at work in his life bringing Augustine to Himself. In the course of this confession he speaks of his whole life including his sinfulness. We find similar prayers of confession in the Scriptures (e.g., by the psalmist, in Ps 50(51); and by Peter, when speaking to Jesus, in Luke 5:8). The use of the sacrament needs to take this double-pronged sense of confession into account; the 1973 *Rite* also takes steps in this direction in its suggested concluding formulae to the rites. In rite one, we find:

> *Priest*: Give thanks to the Lord for he is good.
> *Penitent*: His mercy endures forever.
> *Priest*: The Lord has freed you from your sins. Go in peace.[12]

This last piece of the ritual is entitled 'Proclamation of the Praise of God and Dismissal'. But how often would this formula be used in practice? I would suggest that it is not used because it represents a different mentality from that of those using the first rite of the 1973 ritual.

The importance of this sense of confession is that it both recognises our sinfulness, putting it in the context of God's already given forgiveness, and recaptures the sense evident at the beginning of the third tradition that conversion is the work of God in us.

The forms we use for the sacrament need to embody this spirit. It is harder to change the spirit of things or the mentality behind them than it is to change forms but good forms are also crucial in bringing about and re-enforcing a renewed spirit, precisely because they embody it and practice has its inner, habituating effects in us.

In terms of the immediate future, the only place we have to start are the forms given us in the 1973 *Rite of Penance*. As we all know, it contains three rites of penance along with the suggestion of penitential celebrations.[13]

Given the task before us in the renewal of this sacrament, it seems to me a great pity that there cannot be a more general use of the third rite given in the ritual, that is, the *Rite for the Reconciliation of Several Penitents with General Confession and Absolution*. Where this was previously available it drew a strong response from the people of God.

Since it is not generally possible to celebrate this rite, it seems to me that the use of penitential celebrations is of great value. Their very communal character makes them more clearly ecclesial and opens up a better opportunity to break open the word of God in order to bring about a deeper understanding of sin, conversion and forgiveness. They also offer the opportunity to place the sacrament of penance within its references to baptism and the Eucharist by the creative use of symbols and rituals embodying these references. The most important element in all of this is the public proclamation of God's word by which we are led to grasp the forgiveness of God and the mystery of sin in our lives in a genuinely Christian way. This is the lifeblood of the sacrament.

Notes

1. *General Instruction of the Roman Missal.* Liturgy Documentary Series 2 (Washington DC: United States Conference of Catholic Bishops, 2003) 10.

2. *The Constitution on the Sacred Liturgy (Sacrosanctum Concilium)* n. 72. See Austin Flannery, ed., *Vatican Council II: The conciliar and postconciliar documents* (Dublin/ Newtown, NSW: Dominican Publications/ E. J. Dwyer Pty Ltd, 1987) 22.

3. *Evangelii Nuntianti (E.N.)* n. 2.

4. *E.N.,* n. 20; *Redemptoris Missio.*

5. *E.N.,* n. 15.

6. *E.N.,* n. 15.

7. *E.N.,* n. 17.

8. *E.N.,* n.18.

9. *E.N.,* n. 18.

10. *E.N.,* n.19.

11. *S.T.* Supp. Q8, art 3, resp, ad 1; *Decree on the Sacrament of Penance,* Council of Trent, 1551, in Karl Rahner, ed., *The Teaching of the Catholic Church* (New York: Alba House, 1967) n. 564.

12. *Rite,* n. 47.

13. Introduction to the *Rite of Penance* 1973, nn. 36-7.